THE MINDFUL COUPLE

How Acceptance and Mindfulness
Can Lead You to the Love You Want

ROBYN D. WALSER, PH.D.
DARRAH WESTRUP, PH.D.

New Harbinger Publications, Inc.

Publisher's Note

Distributed in Canada by Raincoast Books

Copyright © 2009 by Robyn D. Walser and Darrah Westrup
        New Harbinger Publications, Inc.
        5674 Shattuck Avenue
        Oakland, CA 94609
        www.newharbinger.com

Cover and text design by Amy Shoup; Acquired by Catharine Sutker; Edited by Jude Berman

Excerpt from *A Child Is Born: A Modern Drama of the Nativity*, copyright © 1942 by Stephen Vincent Benet; copyright renewed © 1969 by Rosemary Carr Benet. Reprinted by permission of Brandt & Hochman Literary Agents, Inc.

Printed in the United States of America

CIP data on file with publisher.

ISBN 13: 978-1-57224-617-1

11   10   09

10   9   8   7   6   5   4   3   2   1

First printing

To my dear, funny, unpredictable—at times completely charming and at times completely maddening, but always lovable—husband, Mark.

—RDW

To my husband Andrew, best friend and soul mate. Thank you for your ever-constant support and belief in me. Thanks, too, for providing such great examples for the book!

—DW

ACKNOWLEDGMENTS

Heartfelt thanks to all the couples (many of whose names have been changed) who shared their stories with us and were willing to have us write about their wonderful and sometimes painful experiences. Special thanks go to our generous husbands, who were willing to let us put our own relationship experiences on paper to share with the world. We wish all of you the best on your path to creating your mindful and vital relationship.

CONTENTS

INTRODUCTION

Attention is love.—KAREN MAEZEN MILLER

The beauty and delight of human connection are timeless and universal. The connections felt between romantic partners are among the deepest bonds of love created on this earth. Strengthening these bonds is a fundamental value for many and brings meaning and purpose to their lives. This book is about enhancing this journey of connection through increased awareness and engagement.

Our intention is to guide you on a path that creates or strengthens your loving bond. Through the practice of awareness and acceptance of yourself and your partner, and the practice of living your values, you can create a union that is full of compassion, trust, deep understanding, and friendship. When you discover the power of being fully present in your relationship—and of mindfully watching your feelings, thoughts, imaginations, and memories—while also breathing life into what matters most to you, you will find freedom and a vast ability to extend yourself to your partner.

Often, we live blindly, without "seeing" our behavior. When we do this, our attachments, desires, fears, and expectations can lead us to react in our relationships in ways that decrease intimacy and even create pain. By becoming fully aware of our attachments and acknowledging our desires and expectations, we can live in a more fully awake state and choose to act toward our partner in ways that truly encourage love. When we stay present to ourselves, acknowledging and holding our fears gently, we are more open to the possibilities before us. This journey does not promise the perfect relationship; rather, we recognize that relationships are works in progress, that the process of commitment includes conflict and differences. However, entering into this process with openness and a commitment to our values also makes possible true intimacy, authenticity, sexual longevity, dynamism, and enduring connection.

We invite both you and your partner to take advantage of the fact that the ability to create a loving, meaningful relationship is within your grasp. All that is required is to put loving (as an active choice) into practice. As simple as it sounds, we all know how easily this pursuit can be swept aside by the incessant demands of daily living. Our hope is that you will keep this book in a place where it can be seen and where you or your partner might pick it up, turn a page or two, and be reminded of what is possible.

Although each chapter is written as a stand-alone section so you can randomly select and take away something from each topic, the book also can be read front to back if you prefer. We suggest you start with the first chapter, on acceptance and commitment therapy, because this will help you better understand the concepts introduced throughout the book. We hope you will think of this book when you feel discouraged in some way by your relationship, when you're frustrated, or when you find yourself wondering why your relationship doesn't seem to be vital and alive anymore. We also hope you will read it during the good times, as a way to gain clarity about what might be working in your relationship and as inspiration to carry on. Mostly though, our hope is that this book will empower you and your partner to discover the richness of a relationship defined by living according to your values.

PART 1

The Acceptance and Commitment Approach

1

LIVING A MINDFUL AND VITAL RELATIONSHIP

Love does not consist of gazing at each other, but in looking together in the same direction.—ANTOINE DE SAINT-EXUPÉRY

One of the fundamental, universally desired human experiences is connection. Whether we look at this from a spiritual perspective or an evolutionary perspective, the outcome is the same: we want to belong and have partnership. Most often, the foundation of such a union is love. Partnership is built upon the strength of loving bonds and the kindnesses that accompany those bonds. So, when we talk about partnership, we're talking about loving and being loved. Easy enough, right? Why not just be loving? Why not just be loved? It's true that this is easier for some of us than for others. Some come from loving families and know well what it means to belong and feel loved. Others, however, don't have that good fortune, with the result that loving and being loved are harder and may even feel impossible. Even those who come from a loving background can struggle with love. Considering all our individual personalities, histories, families, and dynamics, frankly, it's a miracle people can meet, fall in love, and commit to lasting bonds. Despite what might be predicted, it happens all the time. But we must acknowledge one big qualifier: relationships fall apart and end all the time too.

The divorce rate in America, though declining in recent years, remains high, with more than a third of first marriages ending in divorce before the couple reaches their fifteenth anniversary (Wolfers 2008). You may have to go through numerous relationships before committing to a marriage. If you are married, do you remember how many prior relationships you had? If you are not married, what number relationship are you in now? So here's the baffling part: if most of us want to belong and be loved, why do we struggle so much and leave partnerships so often?

This conundrum may have many explanations. It may be that the person you are with right now just isn't the right one. It may be that you are single and still looking. It may be that circumstances and timing are getting in the way. All of these can well be part of the problem. We want to add two other possibilities: experiential avoidance and unlived values. That is, we think couples get into trouble when they are afraid to feel their emotions and to express certain thoughts, or when they do things that are inconsistent with what truly matters to them. Either of these issues can cause struggle in a relationship, and the two together can be lethal. Together, they can be like a poison that quickly spreads through the bloodstream of the relationship and stops it dead in its tracks, or they can be like a slowly spreading poison that painfully squeezes the breath out of the relationship after many years.

The antidote? We're glad you asked. The cure for these two ailments (experiential avoidance and unlived values) can be found in a new behavioral therapy called acceptance and commitment therapy (Hayes, Strosahl, and Wilson 1999). The description of this therapy lies in its name. It's about learning to accept avoided experiences and to take regular action based on personal values. Let's take a closer look at each of these processes.

Accepting avoided experiences means remaining fully open and willing to feel, think, and sense whatever you are feeling, thinking, and sensing. Taking regular action with respect to your personal values involves choosing to create a life consistent with what matters to you. These two processes are very dynamic and require regular effort. But the potential payoff is huge. If you can move through a relationship while practicing acceptance and committing to your values, then you can bring unequaled vitality to it. What we're suggesting is that you engage in a process of holding (rather than avoiding) your internal experiences, while also taking steps to move yourself in a particular direction inside of your relationship.

The recipe for the bond created here doesn't call for cups of miracles or pints of "just figure it out"; rather, it just calls for dashes of mindfulness and a few pinches of vitality. Of course, you'll be cooking for the rest of your life! So let's look more closely at some of the ingredients (both those you want to include and those you don't).

THE PROBLEM OF EXPERIENTIAL AVOIDANCE

Experiential avoidance happens when we don't like how we feel or are bothered by what we think, and then we take actions to eliminate these feelings or thoughts. It might look like this. Imagine that you are doing something, and then you suddenly feel anxious. How do you handle it? If you're like most people, you try to figure out how to get rid of the feeling. You don't like anxiety. And why should you? It's unpleasant. Your heart races, you sweat, and you breathe faster. You may turn red, feel dizzy, or be unable to think. Your mind may say, "What's wrong with me? I'm so stupid. Why am I feeling this way? How embarrassing!"

So, it seems the best thing to do is to stop this awful feeling and the thoughts that come with it (both are internal experiences). To do this, you might leave the situation causing the anxiety or avoid the situation altogether (avoidance). Ah, success! You feel free of the anxiety and problematic thoughts. This solution makes sense, particularly if what you really want in your life is good feelings, such as happiness, joy, and love. So, you conclude, "Out with the bad experiences and in with the good."

If you think broadly, you can see this applies not only to anxiety but to all emotions and thoughts you dislike. You have a whole range of emotions to be avoided: sadness, pain, loneliness, fear, as well as thoughts about being worthless or unlovable and thoughts about failure and contempt. Each of these seems to be begging you to make it go away.

Here's the rub. Life continuously offers situations in which we're bound to feel negative emotions. It's a fact: life contains this stuff. The only way to truly avoid these experiences is to not have life. We cannot escape human suffering. If we could escape it, whole parts of the human experience would need to be eliminated, destroyed, or changed in a fundamental way. We would have to stop being human.

If this is the case, why do we all try so hard to avoid negative feelings and thoughts? Well, for starters, we have been told to do so. Throughout our lives, we've been given messages about the importance of being happy and confident. These cultural messages instruct us to feel good and think positively. Our culture sells happiness as the way to be. But ask yourself—and be honest—how much time do you actually spend in a state of happiness? If you look closely, you'll probably find you fall woefully short by societal standards. Now, apply this message to your expectations for romantic relationships. The story you get goes something like this: A good relationship is a happy relationship. And a happy relationship is one in which you feel happy, your partner feels happy, your family is happy about your happiness, and even the dog is happy! The truth is, this isn't how it works in real life.

Good relationships aren't about being happy. They're about vitality and about manifesting life to its fullest within the relationship. This manifestation can mean so many things. It can mean you and your partner will feel anxiety, pain, sadness, or fear. And it can mean you and your partner will feel joy, love, safety, pleasure, and, yes, even happiness. But from our perspective, the goal is not to feel happiness, but to experience the wide range of human emotions right inside the relationship and still have it work.

Protest you might: "Why do I have to feel all these negative feelings? Why can't I just feel something positive?" Well, four main problems show up when humans make enormous efforts to try not to think and feel what they do not want to think and feel. The first problem is that history cannot be undone. Time only flows in one direction, and what has been thought, felt, experienced, observed, or done is just that—done. We can't go back and make it something else. It's impossible to undo a memory. The hurt your partner created can't be undone. The memory of a horrible breakup is yours to keep forever. Sorry about that. We don't know how to make it different. So, you might wonder, if this is the case, why bother? Bother, because you can do something different from this point forward. What comes next in time is still yours to decide.

The second problem is that the very action of trying to eliminate a thought (such as, "I don't like myself") brings that very thought to mind. Trying not to think about something involves an inherent paradox. You want the thought to go away so you can have a better thought (such as, "I *do* like myself"), but in order to know that thought, you also have to know what you don't want to think. What a conundrum! You can spend a lot of time trying to undo this crazy situation. Or you can just notice that you're thinking and accept that sometimes your mind has thoughts you don't like. It's that simple.

The third problem involves the amount of effort we use to make these thoughts and feelings go away. Humans can get into long-standing battles with themselves in their efforts to escape negative internal experience. Perhaps you know of someone who has done this, or maybe you yourself have. Something painful (such as, a childhood trauma, family situation, or breakup with someone you loved) has happened and you're upset by it. In an effort to avoid feeling the pain, you stay very busy, refuse to talk about it, avoid the family, or drink alcohol. But, whatever you do, as you actively work to avoid it, something else happens. You are working, or *effort*-ing, to rid yourself of the pain, yet it only gets bigger. That is, the more time you spend making the feeling go away, the more energy you give to the feeling. Once again, we have a paradox. Now the pain or memory becomes like a difficult, old relative. You might as well welcome her in to sit for a while, because she isn't going away soon.

The fourth problem gets to the heart of what it means to be human. Humans feel pain (such as, anxiety, fear, and sadness). It's a natural part of our experience. Why we've made it out to seem unnatural is a bit of a mystery. In fact, these feelings can be quite valuable. They tell us when something is amiss or when we're missing something (for example, a friend who has passed away). They tell us about what we value and care about. For example, if you didn't know pain, you wouldn't know about love. These experiences don't need to be treated as such unwelcome guests. In the words of Chinua Achebe (1967, 84), "When suffering knocks at your door and you say there is no seat for him, he tells you not to worry because he has brought his own stool." In other words, you don't have to like negative experiences, but you can have them over for dinner on occasion. They won't be at your table for long, but don't be surprised if they come back again later.

Okay. You can see the problems. But why do we as humans get so stuck? We're not that foolish. We know we can't always be happy and that relationships aren't always peaches and cream. Good question, then. Moreover, the very thing that could help us figure it out—our mind—actually keeps us stuck. Let's investigate.

YOUR MIND IS NOT ALWAYS YOUR FRIEND

The key ways in which we get stuck in what could be called the "happiness trap" have to do with how we relate to our mind. This relationship can be summed up by the acronym F.E.A.R., which stands for Fusion, Evaluation, Avoidance, and Reason-giving (Hayes, Strosahl, and Wilson 1999). If we take a close look at these processes, we can begin to understand how we get stuck and how this getting stuck interferes with our life and our ability to love.

When we *fuse* with our mind, we lose contact with the notion that we are human beings who *have* a mind, rather than human beings who *are* that mind. We tend to melt together with our mind the way butter melts into cream. When we fuse in this way, we believe our mind is speaking the literal truth. It can be said, then, that failing to make a distinction between ourselves and our thoughts is a trap. When we fall into this trap, it's as if we're looking at the world through rose-colored glasses. In fact, what we see seems so true, we think we aren't wearing glasses at all and the world is just that way. For example, you may think "the world is unfair" or "nobody loves me." You feel you must react quickly and with strength to undo these thoughts, because you want things to be fair or you want to be loved. This kind of fusion can lead to a number of responses that are unhealthy for you and your relationship. Imagine trying to make everything fair in a relationship. We don't know if you've ever tried, but it's virtually impossible.

The solution to fusion is *defusion*. In other words, take off the glasses. Notice that you are a human being *with* a mind. Also, notice that your mind contains a vast bank of information that has been programmed since you were a child and that includes all kinds of thoughts—some you know to be positive, some you know to be negative. Some are silly, some are serious, some simple, some complex. When you push its buttons, the bank of your mind can give you information or rules that just simply are not true or are not good for you. This is not to say that this bank of information doesn't contain workable and worthwhile rules. For instance, your mind might give you the rule "Look both ways when you cross the street." A good rule, right? But consider how rules can go wrong. Remember the first time you fell in love and it didn't work out. What rule did your mind give you then? Probably, "Never fall in love again." So sometimes our mind doesn't know what's really best for us, even if it thinks it does. When this happens, the best strategy is to defuse—to see that you have a mind, observe it, and be aware of it.

We also get stuck when we believe our *evaluations*. Notice that, like fusion, evaluations occur in the mind, that tricky beast. Being able to evaluate, of course, can be beneficial. Evaluation allows us to compare, make decisions, plan, and problem solve. It also allows us to do something else: judge. This judge judges. It judges you, your partner, and your relationship. It wields a hefty gavel, ready to fall whenever something happens. Good girl! Bad boy! You failure! You success! The mind has an endless ability to evaluate. Again, the solution is to step back and see that you have a mind. Remember, your mind is not always your friend.

In a previous section, we spent a fair amount of time exploring how *avoidance* keeps us stuck. It is worth noting the cost of avoidance. Most relevant to our purpose is the loss of connection. Avoidance can also be harmful in other ways. When we withdraw or pull back from the world in order to avoid experiencing certain things, we narrow our range of possibilities. We don't expose ourselves to all life has to offer. Our actions can be driven by fear rather than by whatever matters most to us. The destructive thing about avoidance is that it can strengthen responses that limit our chances to connect and belong. If you run away every time you encounter anxiety, and then you feel better, running gets reinforced. But running comes with a cost—no chance for relationship.

Finally, there's *reason-giving*, or giving verbal descriptions about why we do what we do. In other words, storytelling. By the way, also notice who's telling the story. You guessed it. Your mind! Reason-giving can sound like this: "I can't talk openly in my relationship, *because* I get too anxious." It seems that the thought "I get too anxious when I try to talk openly" is *causing* the failure to speak. In reality, however, your mind is having that thought. What if your thoughts didn't cause anything? What if they only seemed as though they did? Imagine if each thought you had caused you to act according to that thought. Yikes!

It makes sense that we tell stories and give reasons to explain why we do what we do. We're taught to do so from a very young age. We're constantly asked to give explanations for our behavior. All that we're asking you to do is notice these explanations for what they are: more thinking. You can have a thought and do its opposite. You can have a thought and do nothing at all. You can have a thought and do exactly what it says. You're in charge here, not your thoughts, not your stories, not your reasons. And this solution is good news, because it means you can talk openly even if you feel anxiety or some other negative emotion.

Fusion, evaluation, avoidance, and reason-giving can all work to keep us in a certain kind of relationship with our mind. This may be problematic if your mind feeds you the story about how you should be happy all the time and then you buy into that story. Remember, you can choose to look at this another way. When your mind says that your experiences are bad or that certain emotions, thoughts, or sensations are bad and should be eliminated, you can recognize them for what they are—experiences, thoughts, and emotions—and perhaps even find value in them.

We're not saying that you shouldn't welcome happiness or that you can't want it. Certainly, we want you to be happy, but not at the expense of living your life. We want you to be happy in your relationships when happiness is there to be had. We ourselves like happiness! But what we like even better is the ability to engage in life and relationships in a way that includes flexibility and vitality. We're interested in helping you learn to live fully, so when all is said and done, you'll be able to say, "I lived my relationships well. I was loved and loving."

Great! How do you get started? We've made the case that your mind isn't always your friend (although it isn't always your enemy either) and that experiential avoidance can be problematic, and we've pointed out some simple solutions. So what more can be done? This takes us back to acceptance and commitment therapy or ACT (said as one word; Hayes, Strosahl, and Wilson 1999), mentioned earlier in this chapter. When applied in therapy, ACT guides people to change the relationship they have with their mind and to make and keep commitments that are about personal values.

ACT uses six core processes (Luoma, Hayes, and Walser 2007) to teach people to be aware of their experience and to make powerful, life-enhancing choices:

1. Identifying what matters most to you, or your personal *values*.

2. Fostering *acceptance* of yourself and others.

3. Changing your fused relationship with the mind, which is *defusion*.

4. Contacting more fully the ongoing flow of experience as it occurs, or living more fully in the *present moment*.

5. Contacting a larger sense of self that holds your thoughts, emotions, and other internal experiences, a perspective called *self-as-context*.

6. Building increasingly larger patterns of behaving and taking actions that bring values to life, which is *committed action*.

Said another way, these ACT processes help individuals contact the present moment as fully aware human beings, in the service of accepting self and others, while also helping them choose activities consistent with their values.

The goal for this book, then, is to bring these six processes to life within your relationship. We explore each of the processes in separate sections: Values and the Vital Relationship (Values), Accepting Yourself and Your Partner (Acceptance), Moving into Openness (Defusion), Being Present to One Another (Present Moment), Shifting Your Perspective (Self-as-Context), and Doing What You Care About (Committed Action). Our hope is that, in each of these sections, you will discover a wonderful journey that brings growth and vitality to your relationship.

PART 2

Values and the Vital Relationship (Values)

2

AUTHENTICITY

When an ordinary man attains knowledge, he is a sage; when a sage attains understanding, he is an ordinary man. —ZEN SAYING

We've all heard it: "She's such a phony." "He's so full of himself." And then the questions follow: "Why can't he see that about her?" "How does she stand it?" These may be obvious instances of inauthenticity, and we may have scratched our heads about how these people managed to get into such a relationship. But if we take a closer look, we probably can find a lack of authenticity in ourselves. It's difficult to be truly genuine in all ways. Imagine being completely honest in every area of your life.

It's helpful when talking about authenticity to remember that values are lived as a process, not an outcome. That is, you continually work to be authentic; you don't arrive at a final goal of *authenticity*. From time to time, external forces and pressures may lead you away from authenticity. In this case, it's up to you to choose how true you wish to remain to your own spirit, your sense of self.

That said, building a relationship on a sense of you that is real and genuine is not only important but, at some level, critical. A friend once complained that "you can never be yourself in a relationship or you'll just get dumped." Her story went like this: "I interact with different people on the Internet in a very real and funny way. They respond back, and we have a wonderful time exchanging quips and stories over e-mail. It's *me* that I put out there; I talk from my heart. And then—it comes time to meet. As soon as I meet him, I feel I must take on the look and feel of the person I think he wants me to be. Otherwise I think the relationship will fail. The funny, interesting me goes out the door and the whatever-you-want-me-to-be shows up. It's as if I become a different person, all needy and pleasing." Her problem is that, sooner or later, the potential partner calls it quits because he thought he was getting one thing and he got another.

The pressure to appear as a certain kind of person can be tremendous, especially when we're looking for or interested in keeping a partner. However, when someone is inauthentic, the effect is like that of a slick salesman: we're sold something we weren't interested in buying. Often we hear, "She wasn't who I thought she was" or "As soon as we got married, it was as if a whole different person showed up." These are dramatic examples of the cost of inauthenticity. Our own inauthentic behavior can cause pain for us and others, and ultimately interferes with intimacy.

What's the antidote? Conscious awareness of our true sense of self and values, and an unabashed effort to bring these to life.

Sometimes during the early stages of dating, we hide parts of ourselves due to our fear of rejection or simply to avoid discomfort. To a certain extent, this could be considered normal behavior. Nevertheless, we encourage you to put your most authentic foot forward, even during this awkward time. You say, "Yeah, right!" Well, yes, we understand it's not that easy, but at least give it a try before you reject the idea. If you're holding back, we recommend that you experiment with letting your true self be present. Be there and be true, and see what happens. Even if you feel a bit foolish, what can really go wrong? It's better to be a fool for a day than miserable for a lifetime.

Authenticity requires you to know yourself and to be clear about the actions that are consistent with that knowledge. This can be difficult to do at times, and carries with it certain obligations. However, maintaining genuine interactions with those you love is honorable. Authenticity not only eases the pain and difficulty sometimes found in relationships, but ultimately may prevent them.

PRACTICE AUTHENTICITY

1. Take a few moments in a quiet setting to reflect. See if you can identify any aspect of your relationship in which you fail to stand for the value of authenticity. Discover what drives this response. Is it fear (or another emotion)? Ask yourself, "What if fear (or another emotion) weren't in charge and I could choose authenticity even in the presence of that feeling?"

What would you do differently? See if you might be willing to take a small action to get closer to being authentic. If you find that you are authentic in your relationship, congratulate yourself!

2. Practice actions for the authentic you:

- Practice discovering yourself, including your likes and dislikes.

- Share yourself.

- Be aware that if you stick to your true sense of self, disagreements are sure to arise.

- Look for the intimacy inside authenticity; you will quite likely find it there.

- Be true to your being.

3

INTEGRITY

I desire to conduct the affairs of this administration that if at the end, when I come lay down the reins of power, I have lost every other friend on earth, I shall at least have one friend left, and that friend shall be down inside me.—ABRAHAM LINCOLN

Living with the value of integrity might sound fairly straightforward. You simply behave in harmony with your personal set of principles. You simply make choices guided by your sense of what is right. If only it were so easy.

Living with integrity is a challenge, even for those who seem to be clear about their principles. For instance, have you ever gossiped about someone, even though you value speaking kindly about others or speaking to them directly if you have a concern? Have you ever told your partner nothing was wrong when something was definitely wrong? What about those little white lies? And at a more meaningful level, how do you react when your personal values are deeply tested? It can be challenging at times to live with integrity.

So, how do you begin to live with integrity? The first way is through awareness. It's nearly impossible to respond to any situation with integrity if you're unaware of your core values or of which actions would be most in accordance with them. To gain this awareness, listen to the voice inside that tells you what is right for you. You don't need a complicated philosophy or elaborate set of rules. Simply let your heart's voice be your guide. Stop and listen, and see what information it's giving you. Your heart's direction is like a compass that points squarely toward your values. It's important to return to this place again and again so you don't lose your compass point.

Of course, being aware on a regular basis can be difficult. Sometimes when you listen to your heart's voice, it can seem to be giving conflicting directions. In these cases, remember that you're focusing on a lifelong process, not an immediate outcome. If you choose integrity as a value, you will always be working toward it. You can build your awareness muscle by slowing down. Allow yourself a moment to think before you speak or a moment to be clear about an action you're about to take. This is especially important when your integrity is being tested. Be mindful of your emotions and careful not to let thoughts such as "Well, just this one time" lure you away from your values.

The second way to start living with integrity involves responsibility. This doesn't mean ascribing fault or blame. Rather, it means recognizing that you're a fully capable being who's "able to respond" in any situation in a way that's consistent with your values. You always have options. If the choices you make are wholly in line with your values, then you're living with integrity.

Bringing integrity to life in a relationship can complicate this process. Consider the situation posed earlier, in which you make a habit of telling your partner nothing is wrong when there really is something wrong. In this case, you can start by talking directly with your partner about honesty and how it could look in your relationship. For instance, you and your partner can agree up front that even if it's tough, you'll each share what is happening for you. Rather than saying "nothing" when something is wrong, you can select from a number of ways to honor your integrity. You might say, "Yes, something's wrong. I'm feeling let down by what just happened." Or you might say, "I'm feeling hurt, but I can't formulate what I need to say about it right now. Can you give me a few minutes?" Yet another response could be, "I know it seems as if something's wrong, but I'm just having an emotional hangover from our earlier exchange. It'll pass, and I don't feel we need to talk about it." Compared with "nothing," these kinds of statements come much closer to representing what's true for you and can help you stay in harmony with your core values.

What about little white lies? Well, they're called "white," because they're spoken with innocence and without the intention to do harm. But even these may be worthy of a conversation with your partner.

Kevin values integrity and works regularly to say what's true and honest for him. His wife, Sara, often asks, "How do I look in these pants?" As he sees it, Kevin has two options when he doesn't like the pants. He can give a little white lie: "Hey babe, you look great." Or he can deliver the straight truth: "Honey, those pants are too tight. They make you look like a duck waddling across the bedroom." The truth here potentially has a substantial "ouch" factor and may even lead to a fight. The white lie? Sara's feelings are spared, but she waddles like a duck for the evening.

So the conversation to be had by this couple is about white lies versus the truth. They can talk openly about what happens when she asks about how her clothes look. If she's really only looking for reassurance that Kevin cares for her no matter what she wears, they may agree that he should say she looks great whenever she asks. If they agree to this, Kevin can continue to state the white lie, knowing that he's giving Sara wanted reassurance. He also can feel that he's speaking with integrity, because they both know that it may be a lie. If Sara prefers to hear the truth—she would rather not look like a duck—they can talk about how to give the feedback in a gentle and supportive fashion. Kevin might say, "Honestly, honey, those pants aren't very flattering on you. I think the black pair you had on last time makes you look really sexy." Sara and Kevin had that conversation, and she agreed to hear the truth, and now he delivers it in a way that doesn't feel so hurtful.

When integrity is challenged in more complex situations, couples can lose their way. These situations include lying (for example, "I didn't call my ex," when you did call), going along with something with which you don't agree (such as letting your partner drive after several drinks of alcohol), and not communicating truthfully about your deeply held feelings (such as withholding information about how scared you are about finances or the state of your relationship). Sometimes these larger challenges to integrity are foisted upon us with immediate and severe consequences. At other times, they mildly and almost imperceptibly begin to change the relationship. In either case, the work of integrity can be difficult. It may mean holding true to something even when others disagree with you.

It may mean standing in a place that's painful and lonely. It may call for saying no to your partner, even though saying yes would be the easiest route. As Mahatma Gandhi once said, "A no uttered from the deepest conviction is better and greater than a yes merely uttered to please, or what is worse, to avoid trouble."

In general, if you continue to stick with what you hold to be true for yourself and act in harmony with that, you'll discover that you have a friend deep inside. This is the reward of listening to your heart in all situations. And it can help others in unexpected ways. You never know: your partner and others may find a voice for their integrity too.

PRACTICE INTEGRITY

1. Take a moment to reflect. Search your memory files for a time when integrity slipped away from you in your relationship. Perhaps you stated a white lie or maybe even a full-blown one. Perhaps it was a time when you didn't speak your mind or state your true feelings. Check how you felt when that happened. What does the voice of your heart say about it now? What would've been the right thing for you to do?

2. Keep the path before you. Find a place where you can take a step closer to living integrity in your relationship. Right a wrong. Reveal a feeling. State a long-held concern. You don't have to set the world straight with this assignment; just set one small thing straight and notice what happens.

4

FAITHFULNESS

Faithfulness lives where love is stronger than instinct.
—PAUL CARVEL

It is hard to discuss faithfulness with light or casual commentary. This value seems to have a seriousness that brings humility to the conversation. This seeming sacredness stems not only from what it means to stay true and build trust but also from the deep pain that can be caused by infidelity in a committed relationship.

So let's start with the bad news. Humans can be unfaithful to each other. Although estimates of how many people have affairs vary widely, one reputable study found that 25 percent of men and 12 percent of women reported having affairs (Laumann et al. 1994). Partners have affairs for many reasons, but usually an affair indicates some form of trouble in the relationship. Of course,

29

affairs occasionally occur even when nothing is wrong. In either case, the loss and sense of betrayal that follow after an affair has been discovered can be devastating. Feelings of betrayal due to infidelity can lead to years of mistrust and anger for the victim, and years of guilt and sorrow can be experienced by the partner who started the affair.

The good news is that, with hard work, some couples can recreate a loving relationship after infidelity. Other couples, of course, struggle to regain lost feelings of trust but never make it. Our goal in this chapter is to offer hope by talking about the value of faithfulness and how to engender it. You can do this not only by remaining monogamous but also by staying true to yourself and your way of being in the world.

The word "faithfulness" is derived from the Latin *fides*, meaning "to trust." The word "trust" is based on an older word, *dru*, which refers to a tree and connotes the steadfastness of an oak. Faithfulness, then, is about remaining steadfast and true, like an oak tree. And to do this is a choice you can make again and again in your relationships.

Mostly when people talk about faithfulness, they're speaking about being committed to a partner. Also at issue, however, is being true to oneself. If you're committed to your own integrity and authenticity, it's more difficult to be unfaithful to a partner. But what does this really mean? Where do you draw the line with respect to faithfulness and infidelity? It's normal, for example, to encounter flirting outside a committed relationship. It's natural to feel attracted to others even though you have a partner. You and your partner may joke about these flirtations and tease each other about your attractions.

Consider how this worked for Reggie and Jazmin. They enjoyed ribbing each other in a good-natured way about flirtations with the opposite sex. However, their flirting never went beyond innocent and short connections with another person. Each remained clear about not wanting to hurt the other. They were very careful about this, not even wanting to create the impression that the flirtation could go beyond anything but good fun. For each of them and as a couple, this was about taking a stand of trueness to self and other.

Tom and Karen missed the essence of this stance. Tom flirted relentlessly with the women on his city softball team. These flirtations included winks, sexual comments, and even an occasional slap on the derriere. Karen tried to be open and recognize that some amount of flirting is normal. Still, she often felt hurt and needed to distance herself from Tom. Tom then complained that it was nothing and said she was taking it too seriously.

Tom was committed to Karen. He'd never had an affair, nor even been tempted to have one. The problem was his stance, which created the appearance of infidelity and disrespect for his partner. For this reason, his flirtations can't be considered innocent, even though he thought they were because he wasn't having sex with his teammates and because he loved his partner. Eventually, Tom's friends pointed out that he was not only hurting Karen but also hurting himself, because he was developing a reputation for being disrespectful. Tom recognized that this was not the way he wanted to be known. His behavior wasn't consistent with his values or with how he wanted to be, even if he weren't with Karen. As a result, he practiced being more aware of his behavior and began to maintain appropriate boundaries.

Karen and Tom's situation highlights the close association between being unfaithful to one's partner and being unfaithful to oneself. In both instances, the same essential value comes into play. This is why those who are unfaithful to others (or even appear unfaithful, as in Tom's case) often experience so much guilt and inner turmoil. It's painful to act in ways that run fundamentally counter to our deepest values. In living the value of faithfulness, it's important to be aware of both our impact on others and the cost to ourselves if we cross the line.

So far, we've talked about relatively minor flirtations. But suppose you have serious thoughts and sexual feelings about being with someone other than your partner. How can you maintain faithfulness if this happens? We suggest the following. First, allow the thoughts and feelings to come and go just like a bee buzzing nearby. If you swat it and run, the bee will get agitated and pursue you. If you just let it be, it will go away on its own. Take caution, however: this is not an invitation to let the bee move in and make honey. Actively entertaining those thoughts and feelings is not the same as letting them come and go. Second, always remember that actions are separate from feelings and thoughts. You can always act faithfully, regardless of the temptation.

Remaining steadfast, like an old oak tree, in your commitments to yourself and others is a legacy worth pursuing. Without faithfulness, you will not be able to deepen your relationships, because it's easy to leave a partnership when things get tough or confusing. Only through practicing acts of faithfulness can you grow and allow intimacy to be present through both the good and bad times.

PRACTICE FAITHFULNESS

Allow time to take a caring and intimate look within. Assess faithfulness and its meaning to you.

- When you think about faithfulness, what qualities does it have? Use whatever descriptors (metaphors, colors, textures, or sounds) you find most helpful.

- What does it mean to be faithful to yourself? To another?

- Are there any ways your faithfulness isn't exactly what it could be?

Gently close your eyes and take a few deep breaths. Picture in your mind's eye a field. In the middle of that field stands an oak tree. Imagine that you are that tree—solid, not blown by any winds of temptation. Just rest in this image, letting yourself experience the steadfastness of a rooted tree for two or three minutes. Make a gentle commitment to act faithfully in your words and deeds. Take a few deep breaths and open your eyes.

5

PASSION

I hunger to engage!
your eyes,
your mouth,
your thought!
—NANCY ROSE MEEKER

Passion plays a trick on us. It leads us to believe that we should have an intensely emotional experience with our partner every day of every year for the rest of our lives. Passion often asks us to believe that *true* love is filled with deep and powerful feelings that are the foundation of our connection with another. Yet, with just a small dose of reality, we know this is not the case.

Relationships founded on powerful feelings alone are doomed to suffer from at least three deficiencies: they're subject to change based on circumstance, they're subject to tit for tat, and the beloved can be overly idealized or seen as infallible. Consider how these deficiencies can play out. As circumstances change, you watch your love turn to hate. Your partner does something you don't like, and you retaliate. You realize that your partner isn't everything you thought, and you're filled with disappointment. Any way you look at it, the end is probably near.

However, when passion is held as a value, passionate relationships are possible. We tend to seek after passion as if it exists elsewhere. But passion exists here with us, in our own home. As the Indian poet Kabir says, "I laugh when I hear the fish in the water is thirsty." In other words, you don't need to thirst after passion, because it's already yours. You just need to consider how you'll bring it into your relationship.

In a playful conversation with his friend Steve, Juan commented that his marriage was "the same old thing." He remarked, "I have to go home to my ball and chain." And before he left, he referred to his wife as the "old battle ax who never lets me have any fun." In response, Steve commented, "I love marriage; I love *my* marriage." He added, "If you feel this way about your marriage, it says something about you, not about the marriage." And he went on to explain that what made his life lively, what brought vitality to his being, was his relationship with his wife. Perhaps you can see how Juan's words were deadening with respect to his relationship, whereas Steve's were enlivening. Steve imbued his marriage with life in a simple exchange. This is something Steve—and Juan, for that matter—can choose to do again and again. Even in jest, it matters whether you see your relationships as being with or without vitality, with or without passion.

This brings us to an interesting definition: vitality is a force that distinguishes the living from the nonliving. So ask yourself, Is my relationship alive and animated or dead and tedious? If the latter, have you forgotten to bring interest or passion to it? You can't maintain boundless enthusiasm for your partner on a minute-by-minute basis, but what can you do daily to show your passion to and for your partner? This can even be done through small acts of awareness and engagement. For instance:

- Listen to your partner mindfully; hear every word, every laugh.

- Be aware of your partner's physical presence; appreciate his or her being.

- Notice your partner's body; be thankful you're aging together.

- Be mindful of your partner's movements; find grace even in awkwardness.

- Pay attention to the cute things your partner does.

- Ask your partner about something he or she is interested in, and then listen to the response.

- Lie together in awareness.

- Feel your partner's hand as you hold it on a walk.

- Learn about one of your partner's hobbies; do it with sincerity.

- Spend a small amount of money on something your partner would really like.

- Ask what you can do, and mean it.

Build mindful awareness and engagement into your daily interactions and watch your relationship spring to life.

PRACTICE PASSION

Reflect on a time when you felt passion (or intense interest) for another person. Who was this person and what was your relationship to him or her? Picture in your mind's eye the aspects of the relationship that led you to be drawn to this person. Take note of the kinds of things you did to demonstrate your interest. See if you can name the activities of this passion. Choose one of these activities and do the same for your current partner.

6

KINDNESS

The smallest act of kindness is worth more than the
grandest intention.—OSCAR WILDE

Kindness has long been recognized as a commendable quality. Buddhism espouses *mettā*, or loving-kindness, while the Jewish record of customs and laws, the Talmud, holds that "deeds of kindness are equal in weight to all the commandments." I Corinthians of the Christian Bible states that love is being "patient and kind," and Confucius tells his followers to "recompense kindness with kindness." In general, people seem to recognize the importance of kindness; according to one survey of sixteen thousand people, it was selected as the most desirable trait in a partner (Buss 2003).

Kindness comes easily when couples first meet. They're trying to win the love and attention of a potential partner, so they readily give flowers or a kiss on the hand, greeting cards with sweet words, and the like. However, as time passes, these smaller practices can fall away. Kindness also can fall away in a broader sense. Not only do actions become less kind, but words do too. We forget to be kind.

Forgetting to be kind may be the result of many issues. It can come from being too busy or struggling with the daily hassles of life. It can come from familiarity or from assuming your partner understands your intention to be kind, even if you aren't expressly being kind. It can also come from pain or anger, feelings that can seem to lead you to actively choose not to be kind. The first two are solved relatively easily through intentional kindness. The last is more insidious, because intentionally withholding kindness means purposefully acting against your value. That's a tough one to swallow, isn't it?

You may argue, "But my partner is doing things that don't deserve kindness!" Now, here's where things get really sticky. You may want to ask, "Do I live my value only if someone else does the same?" If the answer is yes, then living your values depends on the whims of another. This puts you in a weak position that can lead to unnecessary pain, because others will inevitably disappoint you. Why not remain in charge of your vitality and in control of your actions, rather than base them on somebody else's? To remain in charge may prove useful; well-known couples researchers John Gottman and Julie Schwartz Gottman report that happy couples demonstrate greater affection and kindness in their relationships than do less happy couples (Gottman, Gottman, and DeClaire 2006).

Friends of ours, Deon and Robbie, had a rocky start to their relationship, with multiple breakups during the initial stages. They noticed a cyclical pattern. Things would be good for a while: they gave compliments to each other, said thank you, did chores for each other, went to family events they didn't really want to attend, and so on. Then these acts of kindness began to drop off as they got lazy in the relationship. They started nagging each other as a way to get attention. Frustration and even feelings of hatred built up, until sooner or later they broke up. This would be followed by a period of repentance and a return to acts of kindness. Eventually, the whole cycle started all over again.

Robbie finally recognized this pattern and decided to continue to engage in acts of kindness as a habit of giving, even when the relationship began to settle in again. This was hard at times. Her acts of kindness didn't always match her feelings. Yet she persisted and found a new pattern emerging within three days: When she offered compliments and kindnesses, less nagging occurred and more attention was naturally given. Each partner stopped "easing in" or taking advantage, and instead worked to be kind on a regular basis. Now Robbie and Deon are happily married. They look back at their early breakups and are thankful those painful interactions are in their past.

The key message here is consistency. Keep those acts of kindness going. Make them a habit. Letting them fall by the wayside because you're comfortable or angry is a mistake. Remember, too, that you don't have to feel like being kind. Kind actions can be done whether you feel like doing them or not. You also can challenge yourself to come up with new ways to be kind to your partner.

Finally, remember that "the smallest act of kindness is worth more than the grandest intention." Regular acts of kindness—even as small as saying "I appreciate that you did that for me," letting your partner sleep in an extra ten minutes, or scraping your partner's windshield on a cold morning—are cornerstones of connection. Be liberal in your giving of kindness!

PRACTICE KINDNESS

Take a moment to think about your partner. What are some of the small things that can make your partner smile? What kind action can you take toward your partner? Find a simple kindness and do it deliberately and fully. Pick one thing and make it happen today. And then do it again tomorrow and the next day and the next day.

7

LOVE

I love you
Not only for what you are,
But for what I am
When I am with you.
—ROY CROFT

It's the big one: love! For ages, people have fallen in love—and then out again. Philosophers and scientists have written about it. They've tried to untangle it and describe it. Yet, when all is said and done, ultimately you must discover what love means to you. It may be an indescribable feeling or a sure thought in your mind. Regardless, the clearest way to *live* this value is through action. In other words, love is better stated as a verb: to love.

The question then is, How can I be a loving partner, looking at love as an action, not as a feeling? Now, we're not recommending that you forego the feelings of love. These are great, and we're all for them. We do, however, encourage you to move beyond the feeling of love, and act on it. Many couples get into trouble when they believe something is wrong because they're not feeling love in their relationship. This is natural. You won't always feel the wonderful, tingly sensations of love. Sometimes you may feel so angry with your partner that love seems a world away. However, you can still choose, as a value, to behave in a loving way, even if you don't feel like it at the moment. Choose actions that are loving. This involves setting an intention and bringing it to life.

According to Anaïs Nin, "Love never dies a natural death." Love dies because we neglect it, grow weary of it, turn away from it, or plan to escape if things don't work out. What leads to relationships not working out? Treating love as a feeling, not as an action.

Consider an example: When Sheila began dating Jerry, their dating was fun and lively. They fell in love and even spoke of marriage. But then Jerry's job moved into a busy time of year, and though he deeply cared for Sheila, he couldn't spend as much time with her. Initially, she tried to understand, but when a day or two passed without a phone call, she felt hurt and insecure. She threatened to leave the relationship if he didn't do better. Jerry wanted to stay together, so he tried to call more regularly. But then he had to cancel a date, and she felt insecure again. Each time she threatened to leave the relationship, Jerry would get nervous and redouble his efforts. Finally, he had to draw the line. He was feeling anxious about his ability to continue to please Sheila and was getting more hurt and angry about the threat to end the relationship every time she felt insecure. He felt compelled to say, "If you threaten the relationship again, it will be the end. I am committed to you, and you know how much I love you, but it's too hard to believe you would end the relationship based on a passing feeling."

Here you can see that Sheila was basing her commitment to the relationship on a feeling: if she felt love, she stayed, if she felt insecure, she threatened to leave. Each of these feelings would come and go. The question is, what if Sheila committed to stay and chose to take actions about that commitment? This would create a very different process, lifting both Sheila and Jerry out of being dependent on their emotions of the moment.

It's normal to experience a vast universe of emotions when connecting deeply with another human being. These rich experiences are fodder for intimacy and growth. We aren't asking you to fulfill a sense of duty or to resign yourself to an unworkable situation; rather, we're asking you to be loving in your relationship, to engage with your partner and to intend for your love to be known. You might ask yourself daily, "How can I be loving today with my partner?" Or when you're upset, slow down and ask, "What's the loving thing to *do* right now?" Set the intention of love squarely before you and bring it to life. It doesn't matter if you reach a grand experience of love, you and your partner can always find more ways to be loving to each other.

PRACTICE BEING LOVING

Ask yourself, How can I be loving today toward my partner? Go do it! Suggestions:

- Wipe the whiskers out of the sink instead of complaining.

- Leave a chocolate kiss on his or her pillow and don't talk about it.

- Set the trash out without being asked.

- Give an unsolicited shoulder rub.

- Say, "I love you."

- Give a compliment, even if you don't feel like it.

PART 3

Accepting Yourself and Your Partner (Acceptance)

8

ACCEPTANCE IN RELATIONSHIPS

To love means to stay with. It means to emerge from a fantasy world into a world where sustainable love is possible, face to face, bones to bones, a love of devotion.
—CLARISSA PINKOLA ESTES
(Women Who Run with the Wolves)

If you've ever fallen in love, you don't need us to tell you that it's a spectacular experience. Nothing can compare with that thrilling, la-la-land rush. All is well, the world shimmers, and life (especially yours) is full of meaning. Then comes the day when you notice that he smacks his lips when he eats, or she gets a little anxious at dinner parties and talks too much. He watches too much television and

48

doesn't listen well. She leaves her personal items strewn all over the bathroom and doesn't like to have sex after dinner. At some point, you look across your living room, and in the place of your "great love," you see an average person sitting there.

It's common at this point to think that you may have made a mistake, that your partner isn't *the one* after all. In fact, this is when the opportunity to experience true love begins. By "true love" we mean a substantive love that is nurtured and grows over time, a deep devotion that's the product of consistent loving. It's easy to love what we see as lovely, and harder to love what seems unlovely. In fact, we tend to un-love aspects of our partner that we find unattractive, frustrating, or disappointing. But we all have many unlovely aspects. So we need to love in a way that's true for both. This is why substantive love requires a healthy dose of acceptance.

Acceptance can be defined as a "mental attitude that something is believable and should be accepted as true." It also can be defined as "the act of accepting with approval." In relationships, the first definition is easier to pursue. For example, Darrah has no difficulty accepting that her husband watches a lot of sports on TV. This is believable because she knows it to be true. She struggles, however, with *approving* of all this TV watching. Fortunately, a third definition speaks more directly to the type of acceptance that makes relationships work; in this case, acceptance is defined as a "favorable reception."

Notice that this last definition suggests a stance to take, rather than a feeling; "favorable" refers to the quality of the reception rather than to positive feelings about what one is receiving. To receive favorably means to welcome in, regardless of how you might feel about what you're welcoming. When you decided to enter into a relationship, you extended an invitation to your partner to come in. That means all of him or her, not just the parts you approved of and know about. Imagine if the process of dating involved your date showing up with a detailed list of all his or her various attributes, quirks, and problematic behaviors. We can hear you thinking, "Now *that* would be great!" If you think about it, though, you'd be hard pressed to find someone with a completely acceptable list, nor would your own list likely make the grade with your date. Ultimately, you would be faced with making a choice: do I accept this person, even with some unlovely qualities, or do I remain alone?

Acceptance, however, is not about resignation. It's far more intentional than that. When you actively choose to welcome in, you're both aware that you are choosing and also aware that you could shut the door. No one is making you do this. Just as you choose, moment by moment, whether or not to remain in a relationship, so do you choose to favorably receive your partner in his or her entirety.

Perhaps the hardest part about acceptance in relationships comes at the moment when you realize this includes accepting the feelings of upset, disappointment, and anger that arise when your partner does something or reveals something you don't like. Don't be lulled into thinking that by moving into a stance of acceptance, you'll avoid being bothered by these things. They will bother you. You won't like them. You'll wish they weren't there. This is part of the experience your relationship brings. The question is, can you accept your reactions, as well?

PRACTICE ACCEPTANCE

Take a few deep breaths and gently close your eyes. Imagine you and your partner are just getting to know one another. You're at home and the doorbell rings. When you open the door, your partner is standing there with a bouquet of roses, smiling shyly. You take the roses and smile back. Your partner then takes out a neatly printed list and hands it to you. On this list are all of his or her positive qualities. You read them carefully, noting which matter most to you. When you finish, you look at your partner, and you both smile happily. Then your partner hesitatingly reaches into a back pocket and pulls out another piece of paper and hands it to you. This is also a list, but it's crumpled, as if it's been through a lot of wear and tear. On it are all of your partner's foibles, quirks, troubles, and deficits. You read it slowly, going back to those that concern you most. When you're done, you look up at your partner, who's standing still, simply watching. After a long moment, you step back, open the door a bit wider, and say, "Come in."

9

EXPECTATIONS AND DISAPPOINTMENTS

Out beyond ideas of wrongdoing and rightdoing,
there is a field. I will meet you there.
—JALAL AD-DIN RUMI

Expectation and acceptance are diametrically opposed. If acceptance is the key to loving relationships, expectations are their bane. Yet most of us enter into relationship because of various expectations. We think, for example, "This person is going to make me happy," or "This is the relationship I've been looking for." Without expectations, we wouldn't have disappointments. And without disappointments, we wouldn't have the bitterness that can poison even the best of partnerships.

We know a woman, Maria, who was madly in love with her husband, Joe, when she married him. She told us she felt loved as never before, and talked at length about her appreciation for Joe's many acts of kindness. Although Joe came from a wealthy family, both he and Maria anticipated years of hard work as he built a career in journalism. What they didn't anticipate was the sudden loss of the family fortune and their resulting financial challenges. Maria had to go to work even though she and Joe had planned for her to remain a stay-at-home mother.

That could've been the end of the story; that is, Maria could've been hard working, financially stressed, loved to pieces, and enjoying Joe's many kindnesses. But, you see, being poor hadn't been Maria's expectation. She became bitter and resentful of her husband's low-paying job. She found herself judging him and losing respect for him. Instead of seeing who or what Joe was, she only saw what he wasn't. Their marriage became filled with silent and not-so-silent resentments, bitterness, and "shouldn't be's."

Part of the problem with expectations is that we tend to think we're justified in expecting whatever we expect. That's why we expect it, right? However, to our great frustration, we find that feeling justified is irrelevant. Our partner is still our partner; we have what we have.

An inherent part of expectation is the assumption that the other person will share our perspective. So not only do we expect a certain behavior or outcome, we also expect our partner to share that expectation! This may explain why Darrah was so surprised when Andrew didn't seem to care if a bill was paid a few days late. It never occurred to her that he wouldn't share her expectation that bills be paid on time. Struggle ensued as she attempted to get him not only to pay all bills on time but to care about this as much as she did. Andrew ultimately chose to honor Darrah's wishes with respect to paying bills on time, but she never got him to *feel* the same way about paying bills.

If expectation and acceptance are discordant, expectation and disappointment become regular dance partners. Disappointment comes from unfulfilled expectations; that is, you can't feel disappointed without having an expectation first. Of course, none of this is very controllable. Have you ever tried to make yourself stop expecting something or stop feeling disappointed when something doesn't turn out as you had anticipated or hoped?

There's an important skill to learn here: finding a balance between self-rigor and self-acceptance. That is, you have your own hopes, dreams, desires, and fears for the relationship. These thoughts and feelings come unbidden; it's not as though you ask to be disappointed in something your partner does or doesn't do. So judging yourself and trying not to have expectations are ultimately fruitless endeavors. We suggest taking a compassionate and understanding stance toward your own struggle with these issues.

However, we tend to give too much credence to our own uncontrollable emotional reactions, and buy into what they're saying. For example, if you have an uncomfortable, angry reaction to something your partner does, you can easily fall into the trap of buying what your thoughts tell you: "I don't like this. This isn't okay. I can't have this experience." So you turn to your partner and try to get him or her to change whatever is giving rise to your discomfort. We're suggesting that it's important not to let yourself off the hook in this kind of situation but instead to take ownership of your own stuff. Hold steady with whatever is going on internally, while recognizing that you are fully in control of what you do next.

The skill is to have self-compassion and understanding on the one hand, and awareness and self-responsibility on the other.

PRACTICE DISCOVERING YOUR PARTNER

Make a list of qualities you appreciate in your partner and consider to be assets. For example, your list might include "honest," "trustworthy," and "funny." Now make a list of qualities that bother you, such as "stubborn" or "forgetful." Jot down as many as you can in both categories. Now examine both lists carefully, looking for positive and negative qualities that might go hand in hand. For example, though trustworthiness might be an asset and stubbornness might be annoying, the one might not exist without the other. Think about it. Do the qualities that make your boyfriend stubborn also help him to be trustworthy? Is your girlfriend's flakiness part of what makes her interesting? When we're disappointed by a partner, it's easy to point to a negative characteristic as the problem. See if you can discover a different way to reconcile your partner's many dimensions.

10

DEPENDENCE AND INDEPENDENCE

No one can build his security upon the nobleness of another person.
—WILLA CATHER

A vital part of accepting your partner is recognizing that he or she is a whole human being and 100 percent acceptable *as he or she is*. Of course, this applies to you as well, so the idea we often hear that another person "completes" you can't be true. If we're whole already, we cannot depend on another to make us okay.

Noted author and therapist Scott Peck (1978) draws a parallel between marriage (or any intimate partnership) and mountain climbing. Marriage is the base camp, where the climbers find nourishment and rest before they make their respective journeys up the mountain. One partner in a marriage doesn't climb for the other, because to do so would deny the other's growth process and path in life. Rather, the relationship serves to strengthen and support each person's journey. Acceptance, then, involves recognizing that each of us has our own mountain to climb, each journey is a noble one, and each of us is fully capable of climbing.

If the mountain-climbing metaphor for independence makes sense to you, think for a moment about whether this is really how you operate in your relationship. Most of us enter a love relationship believing, or at the very least hoping, that the other person will make us feel good. Because this new person is bringing forth all sorts of wonderful experiences at the moment, it seems reasonable to expect that this will continue to be our partner's function in the relationship. Tucked sneakily within our belief is the thought that this is what the other person is supposed to do, that it's part of his or her job in the relationship. But let's think further about that. Is it really? Who says? If that were the case, wouldn't it also be our job to make our partner feel good, and wouldn't that still apply, even when doing so would make us unhappy for some reason? So, whose feelings get to take precedence?

If we believe deep within that we're not acceptable, it's hard to sit with the notion that it's not someone else's job to fix us. Feelings of not being okay, of fear and anxiety, of pure loneliness can seem intolerable, so we attempt to get out of them by finding a special person who we think can remove them. Examine the times you've felt hurt and let down by your partner, and see how many involved situations in which he or she did not give you what you needed to feel better emotionally.

Isn't it interesting how easy it is to buy into the idea that a partner should take care of our emotional needs? Consider Jiao, who was outraged and heartbroken because her boyfriend, Jeff, ignored her at a social function. She and Jeff were there with some of his business associates, and she felt insecure and out of her element. So she tugged on Jeff's sleeve while he chatted with his colleagues, and whispered, she was uncomfortable because she didn't know anyone. To her indignation, he simply nodded and continued to engage with the others. Nor did he agree to leave when she asked him to go soon after. Not surprisingly, a fight ensued when they were back at home. Jiao tearfully accused her boyfriend of not caring for her, and he was full of judgments about her behavior at the party.

You can probably relate to this scenario, even if the particulars of your situation are different. If we believe that unpleasant feelings are intolerable, we can develop a sense of false dependence that does not allow us to recognize that it really, truly is not another person's job to attend to our emotional needs. Our partner might choose to attend to our needs, for any number of reasons, but doing so is not an obligatory part of being in a relationship. Jiao simply couldn't see that Jeff's emotional needs were just as valid as hers and that he had just as much right to talk with his colleagues in that moment as she did to want his attention. If you allow yourself to recognize this truth about relationships, you become responsible for your own emotional state, including uncomfortable feelings. In this way, you trade your old forms of dependence for a more mature emotional independence that includes observing your emotions, both comfortable and uncomfortable, and then taking actions based on the values you would like to bring to the relationship.

PRACTICE EMOTIONAL INDEPENDENCE

At the end of the day, reflect back on your interactions with your partner. Think about how he or she was feeling. What emotions did you notice? Also think about the emotions you had at the time. How closely linked were the feelings you both had? Notice the ways you felt similarly and differently. Imagine that you *had* to feel the same as your partner did and that he or she was responsible for making you feel that way, regardless of whether it was pleasant or unpleasant. What would that experience be like for you? See if you can let go of needing for your partner to have the same feelings that you do. See if you can welcome the differences between your respective emotional experiences.

11

QUIRKS

Thou strange piece of wild nature! — COLLEY CIBBER

The difficulty with quirks in a partner is that, by definition, they're peculiar, idiosyncratic, and not commonly shared. This means that you're dealing with a behavior, belief, or other trait you may not understand or relate to in any way, which tends to make acceptance of your partner all the more challenging. Shared values, ideas, and behaviors are easy to accept, because they don't require anything from you. Accepting something seemingly foreign requires more effort and greater openness. Many people make the mistake of thinking they need to understand in order to accept. In fact, it is not necessary to understand something to welcome it. Receiving favorably what you don't understand is, in fact, a generous, love-affirming act.

Perhaps toilet paper can help clarify this concept. Andrew made a point of telling Darrah he preferred that the toilet paper roll be placed so the paper rolled away from the wall, over the top of the roll. Darrah didn't share this particular concern, which made it easier to forget to place the roll according to his preference. If truth be told, sometimes she remembered, but because she didn't really see what difference it made, she put the roll in (according to Andrew) upside down. Very little came of this: no fight, no requests for explanations, and so on. But Darrah eventually realized that even though Andrew's toilet-paper quirk didn't make much sense to her, it was just as easy to put the roll in with the paper coming over the top. So that's what she did. In this case, she accepted his toilet-paper preference without having to comprehend it.

However, Andrew had another toilet-paper quirk that drew a different response. He had an apparent antipathy to replacing the toilet-paper roll altogether. That is, he would get another roll and put it beside the toilet but would never place it in the holder. Darrah discovered that if she didn't put the roll in, it would sit there indefinitely—on the floor, on the bathtub, on the back of the toilet, anywhere but in the holder. This didn't make sense to her, and in light of her generous decision to honor Andrew's roll-placement preference, it seemed particularly unfair. She then faced a choice: she could continue to feel that she was right about this, or she could decide to place the roll in the holder and think about something else. Which choice do you think is the best? And why?

PRACTICE ACCEPTING QUIRKS

Count your own quirks. Make a list of everything you do that others have told you is a bit odd or unusual. What quirks do you have that others don't know about?

List a few of your partner's quirks. For each quirk, come up with at least three benefits. Have fun with this. If you're going to come up with at least three benefits, you may need to get creative. For example, here are some of the benefits that come from Andrew's not putting the toilet paper in the holder:

- Andrew thereby provides Darrah with the opportunity to contribute to their relationship by putting the toilet paper in the holder, *and* she gets to feel self-righteous while doing so.

- The fact that the toilet-paper roll is free from its holder means Darrah can unroll it from the bottom whenever she wants to.

- With the time he saves not messing with the toilet-paper roll and holder, Andrew can do other important things.

- Bonus: Free from its holder, the roll can be more easily grabbed in the event of an earthquake.

12

AGING AND OTHER PHYSICAL CHANGES

Generally, by the time you are Real, most of your hair has been loved
off, and your eyes drop out and you get loose in the joints and very
shabby. But these things don't matter at all, because once you are Real
you can't be ugly, except to people who don't understand.
—MARGERY WILLIAMS (*The Velveteen Rabbit*)

In this day and age, it can be an epic battle to accept your own physical appearance, much less your partner's. We live in a world where it's increasingly possible to forcibly fix our bodies to suit cultural standards of beauty and attractiveness. As plastic surgery and other strategies have become more commonplace, the painful, costly message of nonacceptance has become more entrenched. The

63

undeniable reality of aging brings a reckoning: ultimately, every one of us will physically deteriorate beyond repair, until we no longer exist. Isn't it ironic that the one thing that is certain (that none of us can escape), and that we undeniably have in common, is fraught with such denial and rejection? How sad that we view aging as so unlovely and even unlovable.

Barbara got tired of the never-ending self-assessment she engaged in over her body. She said, "I just got so tired of wishing my thighs were less heavy, my legs were longer, and my breasts were bigger. So I worked out like crazy, and my thighs started to look pretty good, but my breasts were smaller. Then I got depressed and ate more, and my breasts got bigger, but my thighs got flabby. I got to the point where I just didn't want to do it anymore." One day while looking in the mirror, Barbara suddenly got in touch with how harshly she was judging her body. She said, "I found myself feeling sorry for my thighs! I decided to thank them for working so hard all these years, helping me stand, helping me sit, taking me up hills and stairs, even mountains. I found myself crying in gratitude for my thighs! Now I make sure to thank at least some part of my body every day." Barbara made a transformative shift from evaluating what wasn't okay to seeing what was there: a physiological miracle worthy of celebration and love.

Of course, we can't just be impervious to cultural influences about what constitutes attractiveness. But if we can remember that these standards are cultural programming, not literal truth, we can better distinguish our values from our assessments. Consider how standards of attractiveness vary. For example, plumpness and fair skin were considered beautiful at one time, while a lean and tan form was considered best at other times. In the Karen, or Padaung, tribe in Myanmar, women with long necks are so valued that women physically stretch their necks far beyond their natural length by gradually increasing the number of brass neck rings they wear. If we were to be beamed into the midst of this tribe, we would find ourselves judged deficient for our short necks, whereas a tribal woman might find herself judged as freakish in our culture.

How does this translate into personal experience? Imagine one of your partner's wrinkles, perhaps a small one by the mouth. Picture it fully. Ask yourself, what makes this crease unacceptable? Suppose you'd been taught that wrinkles are a sign of intelligence, so the wrinklier someone is, the smarter he or she is. Would that change your feeling about your partner's wrinkles?

We know of a fellow, Rick, who used to obsess over his looks. He was convinced he was ugly. When he shared this concern with his closest friend, Dave, the latter didn't know what to say, because in fact, Dave didn't consider Rick very good looking. One day, Dave found himself in yet another conversation in which Rick was seeking reassurance about his looks. "I really struggle with thinking I'm ugly!" stated Rick once again.

Frustrated, Dave responded, "So what if you are ugly?"

Rick was shocked and didn't know what to say, so the conversation quickly ended. The next day, however, he called Dave to say he'd had an amazing experience. "You know," he said, "I couldn't believe you said that about my being ugly. I couldn't stop thinking about it afterward, so I went into the bathroom and just stared at myself. I decided that, according to what we all think is attractive these days, I'm just not handsome. In fact, I'm ugly. But there was an incredible realization of *so what?* So I'm ugly. Whatever."

Rick had an amazing and important realization: his value doesn't rest on how he looks on the outside. Accepting that his looks might not be evaluated as handsome didn't affect his essential worth as a human being. Can you get in touch with this truth as it applies to both you and your partner?

PRACTICE PHYSICAL ACCEPTANCE

Offer your partner a discovery massage. Pick an area—say, the hands or feet—and give a mindful, focused massage. Pretend you've never seen a hand or foot before, and your job is to acquaint yourself with one as tenderly and fully as possible. Let yourself be present to this part of the body, and love its look, size, and feel. Let yourself love its age, its purpose, and how it has served your partner. Be open to this body of your partner's!

13

ACCEPTANCE AND FAMILY

If you cannot get rid of the family skeleton, you may as well make it dance.
—GEORGE BERNARD SHAW

One of the great challenges of an intimate relationship is that partners usually come with a family. Even if we feel a sense of accomplishment at navigating our own family dynamics, having to work with our partner's can seem a bit much to ask. However, the degree to which we relate to our partner's family—every word said or unsaid, every action taken or not taken—is of our choosing. Often, we feel obligated when it comes to our role with our partner's family. In truth, we have the same range of choices as we do in any other relationship. Of course, having this awareness doesn't

67

guarantee that our partner won't have expectations regarding how we relate to his or her family.

The following example shows how powerful the awareness of choice can be. Jennifer and Chris had been married for several years when her mother remarried Jim. Jim was loud and boisterous, but also unfailingly generous and always up for fun. As an only child of older parents, Chris was used to a calm home atmosphere. During gatherings with Jennifer's family, he sometimes chose to withdraw. Although this bothered Jennifer, she recognized Chris's right to take care of himself as he saw fit.

One night, Jim was particularly loquacious, telling stories and seeking attention. Noticing that Chris was subdued, Jim attempted to engage him by asking leading questions about his work. Chris answered in a polite, but bordering on rude, manner. After the meal ended, he went off to "bed," where Jennifer later found him reading. This time she chose to say, "I thought you were kind of rude to Jim."

Chris responded, "He's just so hard to take sometimes."

Jennifer said, "I know," and left it at that.

A few moments later, however, Chris got out of bed, threw on a robe, and went upstairs to talk with Jim. That night, before they went to sleep, Chris said to his wife, "I just didn't like how I treated him. That's not how I want to be."

What's so inspiring about this example is that Jennifer and Chris were fully aware of the ability of each to make choices. Jennifer knew she could complain about how Chris interacted with her stepfather, but also accepted Chris's right to determine his own behavior. She deliberately chose not to ask him to do things differently. However, when it seemed important to speak her mind, she chose to do so. Notice that she still didn't tell Chris what he should do. She simply said what was true for her. Chris, in turn, recognized his ability to choose how to interact with Jim. And when he realized he wasn't living one of his values, he chose to take corrective action. In this example, both Jennifer and Chris journeyed farther up their respective mountains, while growing closer in their marriage.

If you're having difficulty with a family member, remember to ask, "What does this person's beliefs or actions actually have to do with me? What is my job here? What value do I hold with respect to family and being with my partner's family?" Let this information guide you, and keep in mind that you don't need to fix your partner's family in order to be accepting of one another in your relationship.

One cautionary note: Even if you maintain full awareness that you are separate from your partner's family, you still will be plenty bothered when family members do things that annoy you. How can you work with this in a way that takes care of you while honoring your relationship? One thing to avoid is making your partner responsible for his or her family.

For instance, suppose you occasionally find your sister-in-law too intrusive. Complaining to your partner about her sends the erroneous message that your partner is responsible for fixing the situation. Remaining aware that neither of you is likely to change your sister-in-law is an important step. Next, let go of judgment for a moment and get clear about what you need. Try to do this in a nurturing, compassionate way. What isn't working for you? What are your feelings telling you? Has a boundary been crossed? Consider what your values are in this situation. For example, you may value being assertive and having a voice, or you may value being respectful of family or being kind to others.

Now that you're more aware of what is going on with you and the personal values at play in this situation, what choices will you make? Remember, acceptance does not equal compliance or resignation. You can know that your sister-in-law is unlikely to change, see the futility of trying to change her, and still choose to set boundaries for her intrusive behavior. Of course, you may have to set that boundary more than once, and you'll probably feel bothered each and every time you feel she has intruded.

PRACTICE ACCEPTANCE OF FAMILY

Take some time to think about what family means to you. Try not to be constrained by your actual experience of family relationships. Rather, think about what you personally value about family. What is important to you about family? How would you like to *be* in a family? Ask yourself the following: What can I do to honor what I value about family? What am I willing to feel in order to keep what I find important about family alive? What step can I take today to bring these values to life?

PART 4

Moving into Openness
(Defusion)

14

THE ADVENTURE
OF IT ALL

A large volume of adventures may be grasped within this little span of life, by him who interests his heart in everything.
—LAURENCE STERNE

Kristen couldn't believe her ears. "You've got to be kidding. You're telling me David is spending the summer in Italy? All summer—with that girl?" She couldn't get her mind around the fact that her ex-boyfriend, that stick-in-the-mud she'd been involved with for five years, had gotten off the couch, much less adventured to a foreign country. Kristen would have given anything to go to Italy. Why hadn't David taken her?

Actually, it isn't so hard to understand why Kristen and David never traveled. Their years together couldn't be described as adventurous or fun. They were so stuck on what their minds told them that they were blind to what was possible. Let's see how this came to pass.

Shortly after Kristen and David fell in love, they decided to move in together. As couples are wont to do, they soon discovered each other's annoying habits and failings. With each new discovery, an evaluation followed. "He's lazy and has no initiative," thought Kristen when David spent a Saturday relaxing in front of the television. "What a nag—very negative," thought David as Kristen expressed her unhappiness with his behavior. "How boring," thought Kristen when David spent an evening puttering around the house. "Mind numbing," thought David as Kristen headed out to the mall.

When we notice a partner's behavior (for example, throwing clothes on the floor instead of in the hamper), we immediately make an evaluation based on our own preferences: clothes belong in the hamper; therefore this is bad. On top of this, we tie what's happening in the present moment with the past as well as the future. For example, we might conclude, "He's such a slob" or "She has no consideration for others." When we evaluate our partner in this global way, we assign a label or quality as if it were a true part of him or her. Both Kristen and David determined that the other was boring, as if boring were an actual quality residing within them. In reality, *boring* is simply a combination of consonants and vowels, strung together in a way we've all agreed means unexciting. We can't find it within either Kristen or David, any more than we could find a chunk of lead. We couldn't find *exciting* either, for that matter. And yet both partners concluded that boring was not only within the other, but was there to stay. No wonder Kristen and David couldn't see the possibility of adventure in their relationship.

Of course, you and your partner will evaluate each other. That's the way the mind works. What you choose to do with the evaluation is the key. You can simply see it as what sprang to mind when you noticed a particular behavior, or you can latch onto it and hold it to be true. This is where couples get stuck. And it's also where you and your partner can become unstuck. Think about it. Have you ever ended a relationship that seemed dull and passionless and entered another in which you were too sexy for your shirt? Did you suddenly develop something called "sexy"? No, it was the same you, wasn't it? More likely, you freed yourself from past perceptions and behaviors in a way that made it possible to feel sexy. You and your partner can do this in your current relationship.

All this points to an important quality of the present moment: it's wide open. Right now, you have the opportunity to see the past in a new light. And you have the chance to open up to what awaits you in this moment. This is the essence of adventure. Seize it!

PRACTICE ADVENTURE

Pick a weekend when you and your partner are completely free. If you have children, you can include them in this exercise or have someone watch them so you can be even more spontaneous. We'll describe doing the exercise with a car, but you could walk or bicycle instead. Make sure you have plenty of supplies: water to drink, snacks to eat, a full tank of gas, any clothing or blankets you might need, and a cell phone that works. Now pick a direction, get in the car, and go. Your only guide is the present moment. If you're driving along and notice something interesting, stop! If a certain road looks compelling, take it. One couple we know decided to be truly silly and alternate left and right turns, even if this meant rattling down a dirt road. As it happened, they ended up at a clambake. But that's another story. As you go, make up a story that fits your journey; then discover how it ends.

15

TAKING A STEP BACK

Life is not lost by dying! Life is lost
Minute by minute, day by dragging day,
In all the thousand small uncaring ways.
—STEPHEN VINCENT BENÉT

Darrah's younger brother, Jon, and his wife, Jane, bought a charming historic home in Durango, Colorado. Built in the 1800s, it needed work, but they both felt up for the challenge. One major project entailed demolishing much of the second floor, so Jon made careful preparations for this phase. For instance, he made sure he had the right demolition equipment and even rented full-face respirators to be used while tearing down the lath and plaster. His final stroke of genius was to construct a chute from the second floor to the first so heavy chunks of plaster and other materials could slide into a waiting truck.

When the big day arrived, Jon donned his respirator and began work in the heavy dust and grime. Later, Jane returned from her job, changed her clothes, and put on the second respirator, ready to pitch in with this daunting task. She joined Jon upstairs and began attacking the remaining walls with a vengeance.

"Wait!" exclaimed Jon, waving his arms for her to stop. "Don't do it that way." He tried to show her how to break down the walls so the heavy chunks would fall near the chute and the remaining crumbling material would fall out of the way. Jane nodded and continued working on the wall. "Jane!" he exclaimed, upset, "You're messing up my system!"

Jane shot back hotly, "It's okay! I know what I'm doing!"

"I had this all planned out, and you're messing it up!"

"My goodness, there isn't only *one way* to do this!"

By this time, both had stopped working and were standing, hands on hips, glaring at each other and arguing furiously. There was just one problem: both had on full-face respirators. Neither could understand the other's muffled, angry words. They sounded as though they were underwater. At the same moment, they became aware of the absurdity of what they were doing, and began to laugh —and laugh and laugh.

Jon and Jane had stepped out of the content of the words they were flinging at each other, and viewed the situation from a different perspective. They had taken one step back. From this view, they could appreciate the absurdity of hurling muffled sounds at one another; they saw the silliness of the whole situation. In this case, stepping back was aided by the fact that they weren't intelligible when speaking through full-face respirators. However, this sort of move is always possible. That is, we can recognize at any point that we're caught up in the words and in what our mind is telling us ("I'm right!" "She's wrong!" "He's controlling!" "She has to have her way!") and that we have the power to step back and just observe what's happening.

Stepping back can be hard to do, especially when we're invested in the content; for example, when it seems very important to be right. Some degree of skill is involved. Fortunately, this skill can be learned and practiced without requiring a respirator!

Next time you find yourself arguing with your partner and getting caught in the content, notice that there's more to the picture. In this moment, two individuals are each simply trying to get by, trying to be understood, trying to feel okay. Step back and notice from a place of compassion what you both are doing. Your partner is standing before you: what does he or she need right now? Here you are: what's really going on with you? What do you need? Ask what you both really are about in this moment and in this relationship. Consider what actions you can take as a couple to honor your commitment to care for each other's needs.

PRACTICE STEPPING BACK

We call this exercise "Igpay Atinlay Ightfay." Chances are that when it's time to begin, neither you nor your partner will be interested in doing this exercise, so it's important that you both commit to it in advance. It may seem absurd to plan ahead for a fight, but see if you can remain open to the possibility. Your job is simply to engage in the activity and observe.

The next time you and your partner find yourself arguing about something, no matter how minor or how large, whoever remembers first needs to stop for a moment and say, "It's time for the exercise." You both then continue with the argument, but in pig latin. For those of you who escaped this childhood phenomenon, pig latin is a made-up language formed by taking the first letter of each word, placing it at the end of that word, and adding the syllable *ay*. So "talk" becomes *alktay*, "food" becomes *oodfay*, "mother" becomes *othermay*, and so on. "Ouyay evernay istenlay otay emay!" See how far you can get with the fight under these conditions, and notice both your and your partner's reactions.

16

FAIRNESS

Love consists in giving without getting in return; in giving what is not owed, what is not due the other. That's why true love is never based, as associations for utility or pleasure are, on a fair exchange. —MORTIMER ADLER

Few things can make our blood boil faster than a perceived injustice. Some of us get riled when we see others treated unjustly; most of us get upset when *we* are treated unjustly. We place a premium on fairness, and it seems plainly wrong to us when something unfair enters the picture.

The word "fairness" is synonymous with "equitableness," which in turn traces its derivation to the Latin *aequitas*, meaning "even, just, equal." This hints at a couple of reasons fairness might matter so much. For one, we see fairness as linked with equality, which automatically brings up the issue of value. When things (in this case, people) are equal, they have the same amount of value, and we all want to have value. We struggle when we perceive we have less value than someone else, or when others think of or treat us as though we have less value than they do. The second reason is the link between fairness and symmetry, or evenness. We humans really appreciate symmetry. It's orderly, balanced, predictable, and comfortable. How nice. Though we know the old adage "Life is not fair," how we want it to be so!

Let's look more closely at the first idea, that fairness somehow reflects a person's value. How could that work? Suppose a baby were suddenly to come into the world and appear before you. Would you say that it had value? Keep in mind that it hasn't done anything or achieved anything or produced anything yet. Does it still have inherent value? What if the baby were born into a home where, for whatever reason, it wasn't valued? Perhaps it was seen as having less value than another child and was treated accordingly. Would this cause it to lose value? If you think so, how was the value taken away?

If you think about it, you probably see that the baby's value doesn't rest on external things. Human value isn't something that can be subtracted from or added to, even in a baby; it just is. But, as in the case of the baby who wasn't treated well, many of us aren't in contact with our inherent value and instead believe that our value depends on how others perceive or treat us. Then we feel driven to do whatever is necessary to gain that value. Similarly, if we believe that we lose value when we're wrong in some way, being unfairly accused feels intolerable, if not downright dangerous. In actuality, our basic value as a human being is not something that can be erased in any way.

Regarding symmetry, it's likely most of us suspect life is not naturally symmetrical. Our experience tells us it is messy, whimsical, capricious, and surprising. Understanding the difference between wanting the comfort evenness brings and believing that life is *supposed* to be even can help us avoid the struggle to force evenness where it doesn't exist. Imagine a relationship in which everything must be even. We know a couple who acts like this. If she does one thing, he has to do another. They keep an ongoing tally of who has done what, where. However, insisting that the relationship be fifty-fifty causes a lot of strife, arguments, and pain. If one person gets 51 percent, the other complains until something is done to reestablish the balance. This strategy isn't focused on the present moment; it's all about who did what in the past and who will do what in the future.

The hope here is that seeing the essential problem in striving for fairness will enable you to shift out of that struggle and make room for something with far more possibility. How many times in your relationship have you been upset because your partner did something unfair? You did the laundry the last three out of four weeks. You were blamed for doing the same thing your partner did a few days ago. The examples are endless, aren't they? The important thing to see is that when we view something as unfair, it is we who are being "unfairing" about the world. The world isn't a fair or equal place, so this unfairing must come from us.

What would your relationship be like if you let go of the idea that life should be fair? We mean really let go. That means living in the present moment. Take, for example, the laundry scenario. The clothes have piled up, and it appears your partner isn't going to take it on. In this moment, that's all that is happening. Without the history of fairness jumping into the scenario—you always end up doing the laundry, and this needs to be symmetrical—you're left with the simple fact of dirty clothes and a choice to make. And really, no matter how you decide to act, your basic human value will be okay, won't it?

PRACTICE UNFAIRNESS

Your task is to be as unfair as you can for a whole day (weekends are best for this exercise). But don't be unfair to your partner. Make sure things are unfair to *you*. For example, if your partner typically cleans the breakfast dishes when you make breakfast, make sure you do the dishes, as well. It's important not to explain to your partner what you're doing. Just find a way to be unfair quietly. If it's her turn to do the laundry, you know what to do. Your turn to pick the movie? Not today! Observe your own reactions as you move through the day. Notice your partner's, as well.

17

HUMOR

*A person without a sense of humor is like a wagon
without springs. It's jolted by every pebble on the road.*
—HENRY WARD BEECHER

Humor is one of life's great gifts. It's a mystery how the phenomena of amusement and laughter came into being, but thank goodness they did! When humor remains alive in a relationship, anything is possible. With laughter comes lightness, joy, and the ability to make large things small, as well as small things grander. Laughing with your partner, whether it be a snicker or full-belly laugh, is a delightfully sweet form of intimacy. Some of the closest couples we know laugh with and at each other all the time. This light form of engagement keeps them young and full of life.

84

Perhaps the most amazing thing about humor is the fact that we can bring it on; we can make a place for it in our relationships. For several years, Darrah and Andrew lived in a cute cottage tucked behind another home in Palo Alto. They loved that their home couldn't be seen from the street and was surrounded on all sides by leafy trees and flowering plants. After returning from a long day's work, Darrah would walk through the gate and feel as though she were entering a fragrant refuge.

Then disaster struck. New neighbors bought the home next door. One day, Darrah and Andrew came home to find the fence line bare. All the trees had been cut down to make room for a huge remodel. Because the trees were on the neighbor's property, there wasn't much the couple could do. Andrew tried talking to the neighbors, who said they would plant some sort of foliage. However, it would take years for this to make any sort of difference. Darrah couldn't get past what had happened. She was incensed that the neighbors had cut down beautiful, mature trees just to get a few more square feet of house and that they hadn't even discussed such a major change with the people who would be affected. Andrew, being practical in nature, sometimes remarked to Darrah when she complained, "Honey, there's nothing we can do about it." In other words, "Stop complaining, and let's move on." But Darrah wasn't ready.

One day, about two weeks later, Darrah once again returned home and headed down the front path. She stopped and stared at the offending house next door. She put down her purse and climbed onto a low railing of the fence and perched there, glaring at the neighbors' property. Suddenly, she became aware of Andrew standing beside her, apparently having seen her from their front window. Silently he handed her something and walked back into the house. Darrah looked at what he'd given her: it was an egg—a raw egg. She began to giggle, then to chuckle, and finally to laugh full out. In case you're wondering what she did with that egg, Darrah pleads the Fifth Amendment. Just know that from that time on, whenever she came home, she smiled at the memory of the egg.

This is a great example of what's possible in a relationship. Not only can we make space for humor, but we can actively practice compassion and understanding. Andrew was aware of Darrah's intense frustration and sense of powerlessness. He didn't try to change her feelings or turn away from an experience he didn't share. Rather, he thought of a way to meet her and help her express and move beyond the feelings in which she was stuck. Mostly, though, offering an egg reflected his ability to use humor, even in a situation that seemingly had no room for it. How did he know what to do? Perhaps the picture of Darrah on the fence amused him or perhaps he was guided by an innate knowing that there's more to life—like an egg, for example.

PRACTICE HUMOR

Think back to a time when you and your partner enjoyed something funny, when you really laughed together. Allow this memory to be fully present. Remember how it felt to share it with your partner. Notice the warm feeling this memory can bring even now, the feeling of lightness a good laugh can offer. Although humor can't be forced, it always seems to be hovering around with a wink, just waiting to be noticed. So our invitation to you is to see if you can spot humor today. And when you do, wink back!

18

LETTING GO OF POWER AND CONTROL

We look forward to the time when the power of love will replace the love of power. Then will our world know the blessings of peace.
—WILLIAM E. GLADSTONE

There once was a man who had gone without. His life had been hard indeed, and he knew what it felt like to be alone and unloved. He had to scramble to survive and often went hungry. Then one day he had a bit of luck. While searching on the forest floor for food, he spotted an old leather bag. In it was a box. And what a box! It was made of ebony wood, and now it was his. He ran his hands over it and held it close to his chest. Just having it close made him feel good. As he hurried home, his eye fell on something tucked underneath a log—another bag! He was tempted to see what it contained, but he didn't want to risk letting go of his box. After all, he knew what it was like to go without. So he convinced himself that this bag contained nothing, and hurried on. Of course, had he known the bag was full of rubies, he would've dropped the wooden box in a second.

So much is available to us when we are open to it. In fact, you'd think openness would be our natural, default position. We may have started out open to life and experience, but somewhere along the way, we became fearful of loss and learned to protect ourselves from potential pain. Problems can arise when this kind of protectionism short-circuits possibility. A defensive, protective stance can be deadly to relationships. It functions as a gradual choke hold that ultimately kills off all that's good in the relationship, including the loving and generous acts that are its lifeblood. When we let the fear of loss drive us to become overly protective, we miss the opportunity for growth.

Protecting ourselves often takes the forms of power and control. If we feel in control of what's happening, we think we're less likely to engender loss or experience hurt. However, we can cut ourselves off from untold riches. Unfortunately, we're usually unaware of this great cost.

This was the case for Agusto, a known commitment-phobe. His friends were pleasantly surprised, therefore, when he popped the question to Isabel. Despite his feelings for her, Agusto was uneasy about the prospect of being with just one person for the rest of his life. As they settled into married life, he was acutely aware of all the ways he seemed to have less independence. He decided to exercise more control over this apparent loss. For example, when he was bothered by Isabel's desire to know what time he would be home for dinner, Agusto asserted his independence, either by not giving any arrival time or by coming home later than he'd indicated.

Things came to a head after Isabel had a serious falling out with one of their mutual friends, a woman named Chris. As a way to get back at Isabel, Chris went out of her way to be friendly with Agusto. For his part, Agusto wanted to make sure Isabel understood that he was his own man and could be friends with Chris even though the two women had had a falling out. He made a point of asserting his right to remain friends with Chris whenever Isabel sought his support or understanding for what she was going through. Isabel soon learned to keep her feelings to herself and, in fact, began to withdraw from the relationship.

This is a sad case of passing up the rubies to keep the wooden box. Agusto was caught up in protectionism, mistakenly believing he had to defend his independence. He could only see that he was being asked to give up something; indeed, he viewed marriage as the loss of personal choice, and therefore felt he had to fight to prove he still had choice in his life. He was unable to see the extent of choice that was in his hands: to honor his wife, to support her, to pursue a course that would strengthen their marriage. He failed to see that *every* action taken in relationship is one of choice, not obligation. Ironically, his belief that he needed to assert his independence ultimately limited his freedom to choose differently, and cost him the relationship as well. Isabel stopped asking when he would be home, stopped concerning herself with what he did, and eventually gave him his freedom back altogether. To this day, he remains unaware of what might have happened had he made the choice to be open and undefended in his marriage.

Power and control are illusory. However, we are never in danger of losing our power to choose. No one can take it from us. Our greatest form of independence is, in fact, our ability to choose. When we take actions to protect what doesn't really need protecting, we cut ourselves off from possibility. In your relationship, is there any way in which you might be passing up a bag of rubies?

PRACTICE LETTING GO OF POWER AND CONTROL

Take a few deep breaths and close your eyes. Imagine that you're standing on a stage in a huge auditorium. The crowd is giving you a standing ovation! An official steps forward and places an enormous medal around your neck. You turn it over and read "Grand Master of Power and Control." You wave to the adoring crowd. Then you walk about town, your medal around your neck. Everyone smiles at the Grand Master of Power and Control. You have your own special parking space. In the coffee shop, people make space for you at the front of the line. But the medal is beginning to feel heavy. It pulls at your neck and you get a headache. Plus, no one will talk to you. They salute and then hurry away. You're spending a lot of time alone. Finally, you just can't stand the weight anymore and you take the medal off. What a relief! You feel blessedly light. You can move freely again. Let yourself rest in this lightness, knowing that this is what giving up power and control will grant you.

19

THE POWER OF SLOW

One moment of patience may ward off great disaster. One moment of
impatience may ruin a whole life.—CHINESE PROVERB

"I want it, and I want it now!" Well, what more can we say? In our fast-paced culture, we're used to getting things quickly. We even get upset if the Internet takes eight seconds, not two, to locate what we want.

It's hard to cultivate slowness in these times, yet we suggest it is wholly worth it. The power of taking things slowly in a relationship can ward off disaster and make room for gentleness and "right" action. Living more slowly as a value requires not just letting time pass without harried action but also having the courage to experience ambiguity, confusion, and even pain while waiting quietly to see what unfolds.

Slowness can be cultivated in a couple of ways, but let's first talk about the cost of pressured hurry. Have you ever made a comment you later wished you hadn't said? Yeah, we've all done that. It's just one tiny cost of failing to wait, to pause. Have you sped through traffic only to find yourself waiting at the next light alongside those you angrily zoomed past? Oops, that's something else we've all probably done. Have you assumed the worst of your partner, only to learn that he or she was off doing something kind for you? Ouch. These little pressured moments may not seem important on their own, but add them up and they amount to precious time lost in hurrying and assuming.

When we get caught up in speed, we lose the moment. We don't see the world and the beautiful things it offers. We miss kind gestures and thoughtful words. We hurry around wishing time away, forgetting that this moment is all we really have. In relationships, we miss the moment when waiting could've prevented a fight. We forgo the smile on our partner's face and the uniquely humorous ways in which he or she is trying to connect with us. We miss the opportunity to offer or receive love. The message? Slow down.

Cathy and Tony's relationship is defined by their measures of speed. She thinks he's *too slow* to get up in the morning. He hates how *long* it takes her to get ready. She wants him to clean *faster*. He wants to take the dog for a walk in the park *promptly*. She agrees to go if they stay *only* twenty minutes. He wants to see a movie *today*. She insists on leaving *immediately* to get good seats. He wants to eat dinner or he'll *just starve*. She wants to make a plan *pronto*, before she cooks. And here's a funny one: he wants her to *hurry up* and meditate! And on it goes. The hardest part, however, is the impatience they have with each other's internal experiences. He wants her to feel better *instantly*. She wants him to make up his mind *now*. This couple needs a healthy dose of slow.

Slowness takes effort and requires your full attention. You can cultivate it in at least two ways. First, engage in mindfulness. This takes practice and involves being fully aware in the present moment. Gently focus awareness on your emotions and thoughts. Are your thoughts telling you or your partner to hurry? Gently observe the situation and do what's best for both of you in the moment.

Second, practice waiting. Take time to slow down. If you catch yourself rushing, take a deep breath and wait one full minute. Lighten your foot on the gas pedal and notice how you're driving. Walk slower. Meditate. In your relationship, catch yourself making assumptions and see them for what they are. Give your partner the benefit of the doubt. Do any activity with deliberate slowness. Allow your partner needed space and time, and take careful notice of his or her feelings. In some situations, the greatest gift you can give your partner is simply patience.

PRACTICE PATIENCE

Build your slowness muscle. Pick one activity you usually rush through (such as folding the laundry or cleaning the kitchen), and do it slowly. Pick one thing you tend to rush your partner through, and imagine you're in his or her shoes. How would you like to be treated? Consider slowness in this situation.

PART 5

Being Present to One Another (Present Moment)

20

MINDFULNESS

The moment one gives close attention to anything, even a blade of grass, it becomes a mysterious, awesome, indescribably magnificent world in itself.—HENRY MILLER

What is one of your favorite moments? We're not just referring to a good memory, but to a time when you experienced a keen and sharp connection with yourself and your world, when you felt centered and alive. As an example, Robyn had such a moment when she was mountain biking on an advanced trail in the Tahoe Basin in Nevada. She beheld the glorious sight of the lake a thousand feet below and the scary narrowness of the trail. She felt her feet on the pedals and her hands gripping the handlebars. The sounds of birds, a breeze whistling through the trees, and her tires pushing through the gravelly trail were completely available to her senses. She remembers the steady sound and feel of her breathing as she pressed forward in the spring air. It was magnificent! She also had a moment like this when she walked toward her husband on their wedding day.

Having these kinds of moments is part of what makes life so vibrant and fascinating. Why don't we have more of them? Why aren't our days filled with such clear and vital moments? It's easy to point to our daily routine as getting in the way. It can bog us down and seem to suck these moments away, like water running down a drain. How, you might ask, can we have these moments more often? And more to the point, how can we have these moments more often with our partners?

Let's take a look at a barrier that's larger than our daily routine. We tend to think of these moments as "times" that are visited upon us. They happen accidentally rather than purposefully. We are not in control of these connections with ourselves and our world, or so we think.

And yet, what if we could be? In fact, these kinds of moments are available to us even in the humdrum, oh-so-common moments of our day. They're available all the time, right now. You can find them in *present moment awareness*. You can find them when you turn your mind to the *now*. You simply need to direct your attention in a mindful way to what is happening in *this* place.

This is easily said, of course, but not so easily done. If you ever have tried to be mindful, or practiced meditation, you'll recognize the difficulty of paying full attention, even for a short time. Our minds are busy creatures. They like to swoop in swiftly and drag you away to think about your future or past, without allowing you the slightest opportunity to greet the moment.

Take a second to reflect on your own mind's busyness. Notice how much time you spend thinking about what has happened already and on planning, organizing, or worrying about what comes next. We don't show up to here-and-now awareness. And we miss moment after moment of great moments. We miss the opportunity to be present to our surroundings and the world. We miss the opportunity to see the magnificence of our partners.

Fortunately, you can breathe life into this process. This involves practicing being mindfully aware, being present to your partner and your relationship. This isn't a call to meditate on your relationship, although that might be a pretty good idea at times. Rather, this is a call to become more present and to take heed of your partner, to be mindful of him or her. This can happen in many different ways. You might quietly watch your partner breathe while he or she sleeps, or notice fully how he or she looks while washing the dishes or tending a fire. The opportunities are countless, but they require your steadfast attention and openness to both your own and your partner's experience. When you first practice being mindfully aware of your partner, you might find your attention wandering. In this case, gently bring yourself back. Refocus your attention on your partner and let the mysterious person before you unfold.

Don't forget to come from a loving and open stance as you connect with your partner. Openly and willingly let your partner be fully who he or she is, as you remain mindfully present in the moment to this person you love. See if more favorite moments with your partner arise.

PRACTICE MINDFULNESS

Pick a time when you can be alone for a few minutes, but also when your partner isn't too far away. Sit quietly with your eyes closed and begin to imagine that you're as open as the universe. Imagine that you can experience and hold all, just as the ocean experiences the wave and "holds" the rain. With each breath, imagine that you're breathing in openness and love. After a few minutes, gently bring yourself back and find your partner. From this open stance, let yourself be mindfully aware of your partner. Be fully aware of him or her, gently noticing. Let go of any effort to make your experience be one way or another. Simply be aware of your partner from this open place.

21

FINDING BEAUTY

When you have only two pennies left in the world, buy a loaf of bread with one and a lily with the other.—CHINESE PROVERB

An older couple, Shirley and Rick, planned what they thought would be one of their last vacations. Finances and aging were making their trips more difficult. They wanted to travel to southern Utah to take in the beauty of the national forests. They had heard from a number of friends about the majesty of the arches and splendor of the earth's color in that part of the country. As the day of departure neared, Shirley prepared with a sense of curiosity and gratefulness for a well-earned trip. She quietly went about packing and enjoyed the process of getting ready. Her husband took a different approach. He spent his days worrying about what he would take, what route they would follow, and how much time they could spend in each place they planned to visit.

The day arrived, and Shirley made a quick check around the house, then loaded her luggage into the car. She was ready to go. As she waited, Rick ran around frantically checking and rechecking his lists to make sure everything was in order. They had planned to leave in early morning, but by the time Rick had finished his checking, it was early afternoon. Shirley sat in the car, ready and open for whatever the trip might bring. Rick stepped on the gas and complained about how they were off schedule and needed to make up time in order to get back on track and enjoy themselves at their first stop.

As the trip continued, Shirley settled in and enjoyed the view as they drove. She noticed the red-sandy colors of the hills and the odd shapes of trees and bushes. She commented every now and then, when a rabbit dashed across the desert or she spied a cactus by the side of the road. She found beauty all along the way. Her vacation had started. Rick, on the other hand, replied briefly to her observations and commented about the beauty yet to come. Most of the time, however, he stared at the road, troubled over the fact that they were still miles from their first destination. He told himself he would relax when they got there.

Now, the point to this story was probably obvious from the moment you started reading it. But the funny thing is—it's true. In fact, their vacation continued in the same manner, with Shirley finding beauty everywhere and Rick finding a new way to worry about what they might be missing. He couldn't find the beauty in the moment, because he was too busy waiting for it in the future. Maybe you know someone like this. Or maybe you or your partner always want to hurry up and have fun, but are too busy to have fun in the present. Maybe you're so focused on the outcome that you forget about the process.

The process is what is happening *now*. Each moment is here to be enjoyed. And the place to find beauty is here, not sometime in the future or in some other place. It's in the cactus on the side of the road and in the dash of the rabbit across the sand. In the moment when you're aware of what you see, hear, and sense. The goal is to find the moment everywhere! Find it in your partner's eyes and in your time together. Find it in your partner's smile and walk. Find it in your partner's touch. Find the moment everywhere. But most of all, if you remember to be aware and be *here*, the moment will find you.

PRACTICE FINDING BEAUTY

Revisit a sweet memory that involves your partner. As you reflect on this memory, look for the beauty you experienced in your partner. What was it like? To what did you pay the closest attention? Now spend some time with your partner. Pay attention and see the beauty in your partner today.

22

CALM IN THE MIDST OF THE STORM

At the center of your being you have the answer; you know who you are and you know what you want.—LAO-TZU

Times exist in all relationships when everything feels like a struggle. Your partner doesn't do things right, doesn't talk right, move right, look right. This, for the most part, is part of the larger pattern of being with someone. It's natural for storms to come and go in a relationship. Some of these storms are small and pass with hardly any notice. They may even make you laugh later when you look back on them.

One morning, early in their relationship, Mark agreed to make French toast for breakfast. As it turns out, Robyn enjoys her French

103

toast with extra cinnamon—a lot of extra cinnamon. She asked Mark if he would make hers that way. He agreed but thought that "extra" meant just a little bit more. When Robyn got her French toast, she was disappointed. When she asked Mark if he had put extra on it, he got slightly defensive and gruffly said yes. Robyn said, "Oh, please pass the cinnamon," with the intention of adding more. A playful but semiserious fight ensued about how much was the appropriate amount of cinnamon for French toast. "Nobody puts that much cinnamon on French toast," said Mark.

"It doesn't matter," said Robyn. "That's how much I like on mine."

And on it went, for nearly thirty minutes. The disagreement only ended after Robyn's mom, who was visiting, yelled from another room for them to stop.

This was a little storm but a storm nonetheless. Both Mark and Robyn still look back, laugh, and rib each other a bit about cinnamon. Although each believes the "cinnamon incident" was a minor disagreement, they both still think the other person was being unreasonable. Each was more invested in being right than in being aware of and honoring the other's perspective. They were more intent on proving a point than on appreciating each other's unique contribution to the relationship. This attitude can be even more costly when the storms are big.

Friends of ours, who'd been married for just two years, were overtaken by a gigantic storm when, as the result of a family tragedy, they were suddenly faced with the possibility of an ailing sister moving in to share their small home. They had many heated discussions and arguments over this possibility. No one else in the family was available to care for the sister, and she couldn't care for herself due to her limitations. The arguments ranged in nature from finances to who would cook after a long day at work to who would go to the store while the other stayed home with the ailing sister.

Fortunately, the sister was able to move into a long-term care facility, and our friends were able to move out of the storm, though not before they experienced much struggle and anger—all of which had both an immediate and lasting impact. Each felt hurt and misunderstood by the other and would rush to provide the most convincing proof that his or her side of the argument was correct. It took a long time for the two of them to recover. Even now, a few years later, this storm is still a very sore topic. Part of what makes it sore is the way they interacted with each other when they were in the midst of the downpour. They became so exasperated and infuriated that they were unable to stop themselves in the heat of the moment from making cutting and unkind remarks. Again, the cost that comes from reacting, rather than noticing and responding, is evident in the continued hurt they feel.

The trouble caused by big and small storms can be slightly annoying or very painful. In either case, it's a different experience to ride these storms filled with a sense of turmoil and struggle than it is to ride them with a sense of equanimity, a sense of calm. Imagine if you could ride the storms of your relationship, the big and small, from a centered place in which getting rattled and upset is not a worry. Okay, we know this won't happen with a snap of the fingers. But we also know that the practice of being mindfully aware in the present moment can help. Practicing mindfulness can ease the storms of life.

The goal is to maintain a sense of centeredness even when things get heated around you. In fact, one of the original senses of the word "calm" is related to the time when everything rests and is still in the heat of the midday sun. Notice, too, that this is a call to action, not a call to feel differently. That is, you can still feel upset when you and your partner have a disagreement, but how you act during this time is incredibly important and can make all the difference. You can work on this with your partner by practicing the following:

- Listen with understanding. Hear what your partner is saying, rather than preparing what you plan to say when he or she stops talking.

- Take several deep breaths, paying attention to each breath fully, before answering any comment that may seem provoking.

- Practice meditation on a regular basis.

- Practice being aware of every word that comes out of your mouth; make the words intentionally consistent with your values.

- Practice a moment of patience before reacting; choose your response instead of letting your response choose for you.

- When you enter into a conversation, imagine that you're a large, still body of water, a calm lake. Engage from this position of calmness, noticing that even if it's touched by wind or rain, the lake remains still below the surface.

Using these mindfulness approaches can help you be the eye of the storm, rather than be stuck in the storm itself. Whether the issue is cinnamon or a drastic change in your living circumstances, being with your partner in a centered and mindful way can create enough room for you to keep your desired path of valued interaction with your partner squarely in front of you. It will allow you to honor differences and engage in difficult problems from a centered and aware place. In the long run, you may be able to look back at the storms and see the wisdom rather than the pain, of your actions.

PRACTICE BEING CALM

Sit quietly with your eyes closed and be aware of what you hear for a few moments. Notice your mind's desire to wander, and gently bring it back. Let your body feel heavy in the chair; let the tension drain from your muscles. After you've taken several minutes to rest, imagine the warmth of the sun, and picture its beautiful color. Then imagine that you can take a piece of this warmth and light and locate it right in the center of your chest, as if it were emanating from you. Let yourself rest in this warmth and light. Notice what you feel. Rest for a few more minutes and then imagine bringing this sense of rest and warmth, through your actions, into the storms in your relationship. Gently open your eyes and answer the following questions: Could you do anything different when storms arise? How might your words change? Is it possible to slow down and be present even in the midst of the storm?

23

PLAYFULNESS

This is It
and I am It
and You are It
and He is It
and She is It
and It is It
and That is That.
—JAMES BROUGHTON

W e *enjoyed* looking up the origins of the word "play," which is entirely apropos. The definitions were fun in themselves. Listen to your insides as you read these meanings: "to engage in sport or recreation, to frolic, to engage in light movement, to be spontaneous in activity, to make a series of moves that are calculated to arouse friendly feelings" (www.dictionary.com). These feel vital and, together, convey the essence of joyful experience.

Couples play in all kinds of ways. Some couples are amused by dry comments and sarcasm, while others play in physical ways and like to wrestle around. Some find common activities, and yet others lie in bed and giggle about body sounds. All is done in the service of playing, of having joy within the relationship. One of the great qualities of play is that you don't need to work at being in the present moment when you're frolicking. It happens naturally. Play connects you with what is happening now. Your worries about tomorrow and reflections on yesterday are overcome by the joy you feel now.

Remember to keep play alive. We spend so much time in the sober experiences of the day, and in taking ourselves seriously, that we forget to have fun. Once play moves out of a relationship, the tedium of organization and structure moves in and eclipses everything else.

Sometimes engaging in play is just a matter of letting things go and making space for it. That housework that needs to be done will still be there tomorrow. The lawn that needs to be mowed can wait (or you can pay a neighbor kid to do it). Grab your toys and go to the beach, go for a hike, adventure to a new restaurant, or go to the park and play ball. Whatever brings joy to your relationship, do it! Abraham Lincoln once said, "And in the end, it's not the years in your life that count. It's the life in your years." Of course, sometimes you have to put a little effort into welcoming playfulness. That is, you need to make a series of moves that arouse friendly feelings.

Robyn grew up with three brothers, so wrestling was part of her daily experience as a child. Being affectionately twisted into knots was a familiar (and at times interminable) position. Play-boxing and horsing around were no strangers to "the Robynater." When she married, it felt natural to bring playful activity into her partnership. However, the fact that Mark was a lifelong martial artist made being playful an interesting learning experience. One day, Robyn playfully began to box with him, using full sound effects and a light heart. With a smile on his face, he aligned his body and threw what he thought was a gentle punch but inadvertently landed what felt like a devastating blow to the shoulder of the unsuspecting and no-longer-smiling Robyn. Of course, he apologized. After that, Robyn decided to teach him how to *play*. She told him to stop aligning his body and to focus instead on making an excellent sound effect with each softly landed "blow." Now you might picture a comic strip with bubbles reading, "Oof!" and "Psch!" and "Pow!" and "Thwack!" as Mark and Robyn play-box in way that makes them laugh.

Sometimes playfulness is just a matter of being open and ready to laugh at yourself, your partner, and the world. Be silly and foolish. Let yourself feel ridiculous. Follow that harebrained idea. Stop being so sensible. Go for the big embarrassment and challenge yourself to be adventurous. This kind of vitality will allow you to continue to delight in your partner and the relationship you're building together.

PRACTICE PLAYFULNESS

Frolic. Go now; stop reading! Go play!

24

FLOW

Flow with whatever is happening and let your mind be free. Stay centered by accepting whatever you are doing. This is the ultimate.—ZHUANGZI

The expression "to go with the flow" generally refers to the process of letting yourself go along with what is happening, rather than attempting to interfere with what is naturally occurring. We've probably all been called on to go with the flow as a way to create ease during an activity. This kind of going with the flow can be incredibly helpful in a relationship. It can make a vacation, a family event, or a normal evening go smoothly and without struggle. We suggest practicing it as a way to keep disagreements and problems at bay in your relationship.

We also can speak about "being in the flow," which is often associated with peak experiences. Being in the flow is similar to mindfulness. As with mindfulness, the goal of flow is full engagement with the present moment. For example, athletes report being in the flow as the ultimate form of engagement in their sport. They have a mistake-free game and feel completely connected with the experience of playing.

When you're in the flow, it's as if you and the moment merge and you experience effortless action. You feel that everything is aligned. When you're playing sports, you may feel at one with the ball or with the slope or court on which you're playing. When you lose your feeling of separateness in this way, a deep caring is possible. It doesn't have to involve sports. For instance, picture a mother holding and rocking her newborn child. She may gaze at the child, and her attention and actions may be so utterly focused that it's as though she and the child are one, and there's a profound sense of love and caring.

Sounds great, doesn't it? But if this isn't happening to you naturally, how do you get it to happen? Certainly, experiences of feeling at one with what's happening can just show up unannounced, with the process remaining a bit of a mystery. We're all for these kinds of unexpected moments of connection and flow. We wish you many of them, and hope that they visit you often in your relationship.

But is it possible, you might ask, to have more than just the unexpected visitors? We think so. And we suggest it's both easy and hard at the same time. It's easy because it's simply a matter of being present. It's hard because it requires willingness on your part. You must be willing to experience whatever emotions come with the experience, whether they be negative or positive, and you must also be willing to let go of thoughts that might get in your way.

Consider the following example: Megan had a short business trip in Hawaii. It was a perfect opportunity to extend her stay and bring her partner along—a little vacation in the making. Gary, Megan's boyfriend, was excited to go. On the first day, Megan had an all-day meeting, so Gary was free to wander the beaches of Waikiki. Before she left, Megan gently reminded Gary to wear sunscreen. She mentioned the time she had gotten sunburned and it had spoiled the trip. Gary, a lovely olive-skinned guy, shot back, "I don't need to worry about that." Megan implored him to be careful anyway.

Later that afternoon, the couple met up in their room. Gary had just returned from the beach and was all smiles. As they discussed their plans for the evening, however, he cracked a few jokes about having gotten "a little too much sun." Soon it was obvious he wasn't joking. Megan insisted he take off his T-shirt so she could have a look. After a little grumbling, he lifted his shirt over his head, revealing lobster-like skin. No longer able to hide his pain, Gary sat on the end of the bed and confessed that he felt physically terrible and couldn't imagine going anywhere. Megan was mad.

Now, Megan could have said, "I told you so!" and complained about the vacation being ruined, while Gary could have responded with defensiveness and cried, "You know this never happens to me; I don't burn!" An evening full of turmoil would have ensued. But Gary made a difficult decision. He said, "Let's try something, anything, and see what happens. I can't make any promises, but I'm willing to proceed with our plans." This opening shifted Megan, and although she was still angry (and couldn't refrain from repeatedly mentioning the importance of sunscreen for all skin types), she agreed to give it a try.

They got into the rental car and drove without any plan in mind. It was at this point that the most important thing happened. Megan decided to let go of being right about the sunscreen, and Gary made a choice to be willing to feel physically uncomfortable. They both wanted to connect in this beautiful place. They pulled off at a remote beach, which was shady because the sun was setting behind a mountain, and got into the water. What happened next was pure flow. They bodysurfed and splashed. They gasped at the large waves and laughed at their own awkward floundering. At times, they came together to hug and kiss; at other times, they watched one another ride the waves. Gary laughed when a wave pushed him into the sand, even though his skin hurt even more. He shouted, "I can take it!" while Megan smiled and rolled her eyes. They were surrounded by beauty and they were *in* beauty—they were not focused on the past or the future, but were at one with the ocean and each other.

Megan and Gary describe this time at the beach as the best part of their trip. They were willing to let go and let themselves experience. Certainly, you can see how this could've turned out a completely different way. But their spontaneity and willingness created something different. So the question is, what will you and your partner create? When the opportunity arrives, from a place of awareness of emotion and thought, the invitation to choose what matters may very well be an invitation to experience flow.

PRACTICE FLOW

Take a mindful walk with your partner. Let yourself be fully in the flow of the experience. Listen to the sounds around you, including your partner's voice and breathing. Be present to what you see. Feel your feet touch the ground and the breeze on your cheeks. Feel your partner's hand in yours. Notice the time of day and the placement of the sun or moon. Notice your partner and feel the connection between you.

PART 6

Shifting Your
Perspective
(Self-as-Context)

25

A PLACE FOR EMPATHY

Suffering and joy teach us, if we allow them, how to make the leap of empathy, which transports us into the soul and heart of another person.—FRITZ WILLIAMS

The word "empathy" is derived from the Greek *empatheia*, meaning "passion." Further analyzed, we have *en*, meaning "in," and *pathos*, meaning "feeling." Given this, empathy is passion in feeling; specifically, passion in one's feeling for another. It's the ability to very strongly think and feel oneself into the inner life of another (Kohut 1984). This ability is powerful in relationships. It allows one partner, as much as possible, to truly understand the feelings of the other. The inability to be empathetic can lead to real problems in intimate relationships.

Gregg and Jesse hit it off from the moment they met. They had a great deal of fun in their relationship and began to consider getting married. They were particularly happy because they both were in their late thirties and had begun to worry that they might never meet the partner of their dreams. Then, suddenly, their circumstances changed in a dramatic way. Gregg went to the doctor for a routine physical and left with a painful diagnosis: cancer of the lymph nodes. He was scheduled for surgery, chemotherapy, and radiation right away. Jesse, of course, was very supportive. She also was frightened by the diagnosis and what might happen. She committed to being there for Gregg every step of the way, and they grew even closer in the weeks following his surgery.

Gregg's treatment was to last about six months. Just a few weeks into the process, Jesse's sister, Genie, with whom she was very close, fell ill. Unfortunately, Genie's condition was a bit of mystery; the doctors could only conjecture that it was connected to a recent trip to Mexico. Genie deteriorated rapidly, to the point where she could barely take care of herself. When Jesse was called upon to help, Gregg understood and knew that she would split her time between him and Genie.

What happened next makes sense, given the circumstances. Gregg was very ill from his treatment, and Jesse was running ragged trying to care for both patients. Irritations between Jesse and Gregg grew, and their empathy for each other began to wane. Gregg wanted more time and reassurance. He wanted to plan their wedding, even in the face of his struggles. Jesse wanted more time to relax and recover from her exhaustion. She didn't have the space to think about the future, because she barely could keep up with what was happening on a daily basis. The couple began to have full-on arguments. Each felt misunderstood and alone.

When Jesse was with her sister, she complained about Gregg. Although she felt guilty about complaining, she just couldn't help herself. She also noticed how afraid she was of losing her loved ones. She saw that her relationship with Gregg was growing more distant and considered ending it. At the same time, he felt a growing resentment toward Genie and began questioning Jesse's love for him. He felt that he was second fiddle, and unwittingly wondered how he could pressure Jesse to choose him over her sister.

The couple's ability to strongly think and feel their way into the inner life of each other was lost. Both were so caught up in individual thoughts and feelings that they couldn't see the world from each other's perspective. The relationship was about to be lost. Then, by chance, Gregg attended a meeting for cancer survivors at which one member talked about his experience of fear and how it had kept him from relating honestly to others. The fear had blinded him to the impact his cancer had not only on him but also on his family. The man had taken some time alone to really think about what it would be like if his wife or brother had cancer. He was able to access the dread of loss and the desire to avoid anything so painful.

Gregg decided he needed to engage in the process described by this cancer survivor. So he took some time alone and let himself truly imagine Jesse's experience. Two people she loved were in pain and suffering. He realized that her fear and exhaustion must be very intense. Suddenly he was able to see that Jesse wasn't just being selfish or picking Genie over him; he could see that she was experiencing real pain. He understood that his own fear had blinded him to her experience. He decided that it was okay for him to be fearful about the future, and still let Jesse rest.

The next day he talked to Jesse about his experience. This did two things. It helped Jesse better understand Gregg, and it helped Jesse relax into her fear and exhaustion and just cry in his arms. The ability to get into the inner life of one another made all the difference. Jesse and Gregg married a year later. Genie, who it turned out had contracted a rare bacteria in Mexico, was able to be there, though she was still recovering.

Jesse and Gregg's story is a vivid example of how lost we can become in our own thoughts and feelings. We all feel justified in our complaints and anger, and often rightfully so. The problem is that when we come from this place, our actions are not likely to be consistent with what we truly value: connection and love. We risk losing touch with our partner.

Building empathy is completely within our capacity. The starting place can be the same as it was for Gregg: Take a moment to put yourself in your partner's shoes and picture his or her emotions and thoughts, struggles and fears. Notice your desire to be understood and see if you can imagine that same desire in your partner. A second place to build empathy lies in the broad recognition of your partner as a whole. He or she is a human being with a history; with thoughts, feelings, and sensations; with fears and joys, worries and dreams. He or she is larger than this moment in time, just as you are, too. From a place of awareness and recognition of each as experiencer, empathy is possible, which allows intimacy in a powerful and meaningful way.

PRACTICE EMPATHY

Think of a time when you got upset with your partner. Now take the perspective of your partner. Imagine that you are he or she, and picture all of the thoughts and feelings he or she might have. Be in your partner's shoes. What do you notice from this perspective? What might you argue for or against as you stand in your partner's shoes? Do you feel justified? What would you ask for? Now step out of your partner's shoes and see if you experience the situation differently than you did before this exercise.

26

GROWTH

There came a time when the risk to remain tight in the bud was more painful than the risk it took to blossom. —ANAÏS NIN

Growth can be thought of as those moments in time when you make large (or even small) changes in your knowledge and way of viewing the world. Your lens on life shifts, and you experience a sense of development, a sense of new understanding. Mostly, that growth is measured in terms of the external world. Here, we want to turn the lens around and target growth of a more internal nature; that is, the growth of your experiences and the place in which they're held. As your life continues, you gain more experience. You have more memories. You have more complex and varied thoughts. Your emotions, once simple, become more intricate and involved. Where are all of these experiences contained? We suggest that it is within a context that is expansive and able to hold all of the experiences of your life. This context is *you*.

You are the one who has had all these experiences, who is having one in this moment. In this sense, you are the place in which all of your experiences are held and played out. As you age, you can grow and continue to hold all of your experiences. You can contain them all. Think about all of the memories you've had and all of the emotions you've felt. Think about how your thoughts have changed and how much more you know now than you once knew. The number of experiences you can have is without limit. You *are* limitless in this way. If you were to live ninety years or two hundred years, you would continue to expand and be able to hold your full experience. The wonderful thing about this type of growth, this capacity, is that we have so much room for experience that even the difficult struggles can be held within it. There's space for it all, both the pain and the joy.

One of the problematic aspects of our culture is that it often asks us to keep only the positive; that is, to feel good, think "good," be good. It asks us to eliminate painful experiences and only welcome the good stuff. This is worth contemplating. Does it make sense only to have the good? Let's look at this. You have the capacity to feel pain, and perhaps this capacity isn't a terrible thing. Imagine if you never felt pain. Sounds good, doesn't it? But if you never felt pain, you'd miss out on much of what actually brings vitality to life. You wouldn't miss people when they left your life. You wouldn't feel upset about the deaths of your relatives and friends. For that matter, you might not even care to have relationships at all. Pain is not our enemy. In fact, it shows us what matters in life. And we have the capacity to experience it, just like all the other experiences we have and will have.

This is great news for relationships. It means both you and partner can experience the range of emotions available to humans, the good and the so-called bad. You each have limitless space, your *selves*, to hold all of it. You have the room for the difficult and the easy. This knowledge holds much freedom.

Let's look more closely at what this means. It doesn't mean everything painful that happens is automatically acceptable. We would never want you to stay in an abusive relationship and make space for that. We also would not want you to be in a relationship that is so filled with pain that you never experience anything else. You don't have to use this capacity to accept bad situations. As you make choices about what you value, however, you can accept specific painful thoughts and feelings. And you can accept your partner's painful thoughts and emotions, too.

This particular type of growth is wonderful when you recognize all the experiences you can potentially share with your partner. Each of you will expand, and you'll be doing it together. All you encounter as a couple is also held by each of you as individuals. This can be a real advantage when you and your partner are struggling. It's comforting to know that you can hold this struggle, even if it's a repeat. Remember, you have the capacity.

Jan enjoys spending time with her family at Christmas. Her husband, Craig, does not. He would much rather stay home. Jan doesn't get to see her family often, so after a bit of discussion, they usually decide to go. Craig finds the expectations of Jan's family especially hard. They expect the couple to spend all of their short visit interacting with the family. Craig gets upset about this and ends up angry at Jan for dragging him along to another family event. Jan gets upset that Craig is upset, and the trip turns into a struggle.

Here's how the expansive sense of self came in handy for them. They each recognized this situation as a challenge and, rather than remaining upset and demanding toward each other, made a choice to accept each other's and their own experiences. Craig accepted Jan's desire and need to visit her family, and Jan accepted Craig's desire and need to not spend every moment with her family. Now when they visit, Jan knows that Craig will spend some time by himself. She feels anxious about it, because it's hard to explain to her family; however, she recognizes this anxiety and welcomes it, because it allows her to be with her family. Craig accepts that his wife won't be very available during the visit. He also accepts the feelings that arise when he thinks about Jan's family not understanding his desire to spend time alone. By accepting all aspects of this complex experience, the struggle during their visits has been substantially reduced.

Our hope is that you'll be able to connect to this place of growth, recognizing that you each hold an "eternal" capacity to think and feel and sense—a capacity to be accepting of all that you hold.

PRACTICE GROWTH

Take time to notice your capacity to continually grow in experience. Sit quietly and become aware of your breathing. After a few moments, turn your attention to your mind's eye. See if you can contact the boundarylessness of self. Think about your memories and notice how they stretch back in time and how, for as long you live, you'll continue to create more. Notice the millions of thoughts you've had in your lifetime and be aware of how you continue to create more every minute. Be aware of your emotions and notice that your capacity to experience emotion will always be there. Notice also that both you and your partner have this capacity. Sit in this sense of boundarylessness for a period of time and then come back to the room.

27

SACRED SPACE

Your sacred space is where you can find yourself again and again.
—JOSEPH CAMPBELL

Have you ever felt completely connected to yourself, another, and the world? Have you ever found yourself filled with compassion and able to feel loving toward nearly anyone? Some might describe this as a peaceful and gentle moment. Others might describe it as a sense of self that is larger than the world, but that's still able to join with the world. These moments are all too rare. They can be elusive, especially if you go looking for them.

The first question that arises is, where are these moments experienced? We think they are experienced by a larger sense of us that can experience these events yet is more than any single event. In chapter 1, we called this larger sense *self-as-context*. In some ways, we might call this space sacred. That is, as long as we're alive, it is a dedicated space for our experience. "Sacred" literally means set apart. This space is set apart in the sense that words cannot be it or describe it, because this space contains the words and yet is not the words themselves. It is set apart, because it's not emotion but contacts an emotion when it is felt. This space is set apart, because it's not a memory but, rather, the space wherein memory occurs. This set-apart space is only captured in our observing of moment-to-moment experience, as part of the process of living. This sacred space is *being*.

When we're in contact with being, we go beyond the mind and become more truly present in our life and relationships. In this place, we're free from evaluation and judgment, and others are free from the same. We're loosened from the grip of censorship and the plague that mind can be. We can interact more openly with the world and those we love. Our list making, organizing, planning, creating, discussing, and story making all can be observed for what they are: thinking. We're liberated to connect from a place that's at our core rather than from our mind.

Relating to others mind to mind is inevitable, and is what we do most of the time. Unfortunately, a good deal of this chatter keeps us from interacting in ways that clearly and simply come from choices of the heart. When we're simply being and following our heartfelt values, our relationships can be threaded with kindness, and the cloth of intimacy can be sewn.

The next question we ask is, is there a way to gain greater access to this sacred place? The answer is a tentative yes. Remember, we said that seeking it might actually prevent us from accessing it. This is the case when the seeking is forceful. If you try to force your way into this spot, the place of just being will be lost. Forcing being isn't being. Rather, being is a process of cultivating awareness, of gently recognizing that our *self* is larger than our mind and thoughts, and can observe those experiences.

Practicing mindfulness, meditating, and observing the moment are all ways to foster access to the sacred space. When we contact being and recognize the being of others, we can form a steady connection with our partner. We can hold our partner in deep appreciation, for his or her set-apart space, or sacred space, too.

PRACTICE HONORING SACRED SPACE

Sit quietly and observe your breathing. Continue to do this for a period of time. Then imagine you are standing in a beautiful field that stretches out in all directions. You cannot see the edges of this field; it's too vast. It's serene and filled with life. Grass and flowers gently sway in the breeze, and bumblebees lazily make their way around. Picture this field as untouchable, because you've dedicated it as sacred. Let yourself rest in this sacred space. Let yourself connect to this untouchable field as if it's you.

When you're able to connect to the vast experience that is you—this sacred field of the self—what do you notice about your relationships? From this place, how do you relate to you partner?

28

BEING

When I dare to be powerful, to use my strength in the service of my vision, then it becomes less and less important whether I am afraid.
—AUDRE LORDE

The content of our life is played out in the context of our being. In this section, we've been exploring what this means. For example, it means we need not be defined by our thoughts, feelings, roles, or memories. We are larger than them. And this larger sense of wholeness of being can interact with the world in many ways.

We don't, however, always do this automatically. Often, we get caught in relatively limited roles. This was the case for Raj and Sarla. They each played certain roles in their relationship. Sarla played the role of the responsible wife and mother. She made sure the bills were paid on time, organized the home, and did the shopping. She made sure the household functioned smoothly. Raj, on the other hand, played the role of fun-loving guy. He always was ready to put off what needed to be done today till tomorrow. With these roles, their relationship generally moved forward without a problem. However, arguments occurred when Sarla complained that Raj needed to take more responsibility. He complained that Sarla was trying to make him into something he wasn't. He feared she was trying to steal his playfulness and sense of self. Neither recognized that he or she was playing a role. They both were so glued to the role that they didn't notice a larger sense of self that's beyond mere roles. They failed to recognize their larger being.

If this couple had recognized the roles they were in, they might've been able to choose different ways to be in their relationship. The ability to choose from the place of self-as-context, rather than from the place of content (or what keeps us stuck in a role), points to the power of living from a larger perspective. Imagine that Raj and Sarla decide to intentionally exaggerate their roles. He exaggerates by acting like a little boy and stamping his feet when asked to do something, and she exaggerates by taking control of everything and coddling Raj as that little boy. In recognizing that they both can choose to step *into* their roles more intensively, they also recognize that they can step *out* of their roles. This discovery opens up many new possibilities. It frees them to take on new roles without losing who their "being" truly is: an experiencer who is much larger than any particular role. This, in turn, allows them to interact in ways that strengthen the relationship rather than create frustration and resentment.

This kind of shift can occur not just with roles but also in other areas. For instance, it can be helpful when we find ourselves judging a partner. Most of us want to decrease our judgments of others, but still find ourselves being critical, especially in our close relationships. We might think our partner is being insensitive or unkind. We might judge him or her as demanding or uncaring. The key is recognition of a larger perspective. Having the recognition that we're engaged in judging, while others are judging us, and that all these judgments come and go, can create the space for us to let go of them. Taking this larger perspective and viewing ourselves as the experiencer, rather than as the object of experience, can also affect how we relate to the emotions, memories, and sensations that arise on a moment-by-moment basis in a relationship. We can pause just long enough to recognize that each experience is held in a context. This context is whole and solid, and it's larger than any individual experience. From this perspective, we can live in the center of our own lives and also connect to that same center in our partner.

PRACTICE BEING

Pick a role that you play in your partnership. Describe this role to yourself. Exaggerate the role in your imagination. Pretend that you have stepped into this role and are fully on stage. Embellish and amplify the role. Then pick another role and do the same. Notice how you can move in and out of these roles while still remaining the same. You are the one playing the roles. What does this larger sense of you want for the relationship? What kind of strength does this sense of you bring to building a great relationship?

29

ENLIGHTENMENT

There are many paths to enlightenment. Be sure to take one with a heart. —LAO-TZU

Ahh! Enlightenment, that blessed state in which an individual transcends desire and suffering. Just as the spiritual journey to enlightenment calls to the individual to remain open and rise above the limits of mind, so does relationship call to the couple to remain open and transcend the challenges of mind. This path of exploration and invitation begins with the self. This is a self that's engaged and connected to the vitality available in every moment.

This journey is about expanding the love within a partnership. It's not about changing the other. This is an important distinction. Sometimes one or both partners become fixed on changing the other. The relationship becomes about the effort to make the partner into someone else. You can hear this in conversations when one partner says, "I wish you…" The wish could reflect an attachment to being more thoughtful, kinder, gentler, or more sincere. It also could be an attachment to *not* being something, such as "I wish he weren't so distant" or "I wish she wouldn't talk so much." If you think more broadly about what these statements mean, you can see that what's being said at such moments is "I can love you when you're someone else." In other words, "I can love you when you're more gentle and sincere" or "I can love you when you talk less." This kind of insistence on change can be damaging, particularly when it's about your partner's character.

In the early stages of their relationship, Diane wanted Diego to stop joking so much. Diego was a bit of a character and liked to play tricks and tell funny stories. Diane thought this was childish and would lose her smile and fold her arms whenever Diego started with his teasing, even if it wasn't directed at her. Diane attempted to manipulate Diego with her sullen behavior, because she couldn't accept him for who he was.

When we bring transcendence to our relationship, we accept our partner as he or she is—with all the flaws and eccentricities, all the faults and idiosyncrasies. We also accept all of our partner's glorious and wonderful traits, too. In this case, we might ask Diane if she would be willing to look at Diego as a whole, rather than focus on one seemingly annoying trait. We'd suggest that she examine her attachments. That is, she was attached to the idea of marrying a sophisticated guy, someone she could take to parties without worrying about how he might appear. She was attached to the idea of being involved with a charming man who would never look foolish. Then she met Diego and fell in love. However, she was convinced that she could change his silly behavior and make him into her idea. But this wasn't Diego. At first he felt ashamed when Diane folded her arms and stopped smiling. Sometimes he left the room; at other times, he tried to joke more with her, only making the situation worse. Most problematic for the relationship was when he became angry and withdrew (and we can't say we blame him).

Allowing the image of who we think our partner should be to dictate how we interact with him or her is tantamount to abdicating our choice. Our attachment gets to pick how we will be with our partner. Enlightenment in a situation like this involves seeing our various attachments for what they are, and then gently kissing them good-bye. Letting go of these preconceived notions frees us to love our partner for who he or she is. This is a more fundamental and compassionate love.

Transcendence in relationships also allows us to take an enlightened view of change. Partnerships go through hundreds, even thousands, of changes. Loss and growth are all part of the process. When we get stuck in not accepting loss or growth, we contract in our relationship rather than expand.

Dale enjoyed hiking with his wife, Sandra, on Sundays. They both came to cherish these walks in the hills near their home. Then Sandra had a biking accident in which she hurt her knee, and was no longer able to hike. Because she valued this time with Dale, she wanted to find an activity to replace hiking. Dale, however, was attached to being outdoors and didn't want to make a switch. So Sandra signed up to volunteer at the local hospital on Sundays while Dale was hiking.

On his first hike without Sandra, Dale missed their experience together and began to plot ways to get his wife hiking again. He planned out her exercise routine and the pace of their hike. He thought about how many stops they would make and how he would verbally support her if she felt too much pain. Later that day, Dale proposed his great idea and was surprised when Sandra said, "No, thank you." He couldn't believe she didn't want to participate in his new plan. Sandra, however, had thoroughly enjoyed her volunteering and committed to it for the next three months. She told Dale she had found a rewarding activity that wasn't painful to her knee.

Here, Dale's enlightenment was to let go of his attachment to things staying the same—to be open and willing to experience change and loss. Dale could've come to resent Sandra's volunteering and felt abandoned on Sundays. However, he was able to let go of his attachment to having her join him. From an open, loving place, he fully supported her new endeavor while continuing to enjoy his hikes.

Letting go of attachments on your path to expanding the love in your partnership requires recognizing and being willing to experience all that arises. It means feeling the anxiety of your partner's flaws and the pain of loss and change, and then choosing love anyway. As you transcend your ideas and feelings, you can increasingly choose to take actions that are about loving your partner.

PRACTICE ENLIGHTENMENT

Think of an attachment, such as a wish you have about how your partner could be or something you want your partner to change. Close your eyes and form an image of this attachment. What does it look like and what does it do that you approve of or support? After you've spent a short time thinking about this image and its effect, imagine you are standing with the image next to the door of your home. Give the image a kiss good-bye on the cheek or a handshake, and imagine it walking out the door. Let the attachment go.

30

RELATING FROM A PLACE OF WHOLENESS

It's a great view from here. I am having the time of my life.
—MICHAEL P. ANDERSON

One of the main things that happens when we hold our thoughts to be literally true is a kind of melting together. We believe that what is said in our mind is who we are in our being. For instance, if you have the thought that you're a worthless person, you find yourself believing that you're worthless and acting in ways consistent with that thought (for example, staying out of relationships for fear of rejection, or believing that friends only like you for what you can give them). From this place, the thought of worthlessness is problematic. It seems that you should rush to fix it, that you should work at thinking you're okay and aren't in fact, worthless. The issue gets even stickier. If you're working to make sure you aren't worthless, you have to buy into the idea that you are worthless. Why else work to create the opposite? A paradox is set in motion that can't be fixed by finally believing you are worthwhile.

Now, suppose you could approach this another way. Imagine that you are a universe and all your thoughts, even those that say you're worthless, are the stars in it. The universe contains stars, yet it is not defined by those stars. Similarly, your mind contains thoughts, but you aren't defined by them. The thought "I am worthless" is a set of words with a particular set of meanings. "I am worthless" is as much a thought as "I am worthwhile." Can you look at your thoughts and gently observe them for what they are: just thoughts. The same is true for emotions, sensations, and memories. These experiences are like stars held by the universe.

From this place of being larger than your thoughts and feelings, larger than individual stars, notice that the universe isn't broken. It is whole—as are you. You are a whole being who experiences thoughts, feelings, and sensations. You are the experiencer, not what is experienced. The word "whole" means in perfect condition. You are in perfect condition even if one star, or several, says, "You are worthless."

Now imagine that you are this universe, holding these thoughts and feelings, and you meet another universe holding his or her thoughts and feelings. You can relate to this person from a place of wholeness, simultaneously recognizing his or her wholeness. When you relate to someone from this place and he or she does the same with you, then the two of you can exist in a profound sense of reciprocity. When you can regard the other in the same way you regard yourself—intact (not destroyed by a "bad" thought or difficult feeling)—you come to a profound place of acceptance.

Dana valued her relationship with Todd. However, she quietly nursed the idea that she was damaged because she'd been abused as a child. She had a feeling of brokenness that interfered with her ability to be herself with Todd. She didn't believe he could accept her as she was. She put on a smile and tried to hide her damage. This usually took the form of overcompensation. She boasted about how she'd accomplished a task more quickly than others had or bragged about the quality of her work. She thought this gave her the appearance of being okay. Although Todd liked Dana, he found her behavior a turnoff and eventually ended the relationship. Thus, her feeling of being damaged was confirmed. She determined to try harder next time and *really* prove that she was worthwhile. You can anticipate the terrible cycle in which Dana will find herself.

Dana, in her childhood, learned the thought that she was damaged. This simple piece of childhood programming then dictated her life. The battle to make herself not be damaged actually contributed to her continued feeling of the same. Now, given that Dana will probably never be rid of the thought "I'm damaged"—no amount of boasting or bragging will undo it—perhaps she can develop a different relationship with her thoughts. What if Dana could see the thought as a thought, nothing more. She could hold the thought and gently observe it, without making any effort to make it disappear. If she is larger than the thought—it is only one star among billions—then she could step out of the battle with it. The star is not the universe. From this place of wholeness, she could relate to Todd in a very different way, and no longer make the choice to impress him with bragging. Rather, as a chosen stance, she could interact with him in a manner that's consistent with complete acceptance of self.

If we draw from this example, we see that not only are we a vast universe with untold stars, but so are others. Relating to a partner from this whole and perfect place allows us to get unhooked from the stars of particular thoughts, memories, and experiences. As we do this together, we create the context for a powerful and compassionate love.

PRACTICE WHOLENESS

Close your eyes and observe your breathing. Imagine the vastness of the universe and all the stars in it. Picture yourself as that universe and gently let yourself be present to the stars. Stay with this image for a few minutes. Then picture your partner as a universe, too. Notice how he or she is timeless and whole. How do you relate as these two universes?

PART 7

Doing What You Care About (Committed Action)

31

COMMITTED ACTION
IN RELATIONSHIPS

Remember, people will judge you by your actions, not your intentions.
You may have a heart of gold, but so does a hard-boiled egg.
—NAVJOT SINGH SIDHU

The challenge of writing about committed action is to convey how crucial this is to living a valued life. In terms of relationships, it is committed action that is the heart and soul of a loving and vital partnership.

Before moving more fully into exploring committed action, let's begin by considering the meaning of commitment. Used widely and often, this term is generally considered to belong in the stack of good attributes for human beings. It's good to be committed.

Commitment leads to success, and so on. In fact, the true value of commitment has almost become lost in its hype. Most essentially, commitment reflects the human ability to bring into existence that which matters.

Commitment can be tricky. Imagine this scenario. Your partner has just told you how upset she is that you made fun of her in public the other day. Apologetically you say, "You're right, that wasn't cool of me to do. I promise I won't do it again." Right there, in that moment, much is on the line. If you don't have any intention behind your promise, it's as though a puff of air escaped your lips and is floating away on the wind, empty and without import. If, however, intention comes with the promise, you're at the start of a journey full of possibility. Most of us lose sight of, or perhaps never understand, the power of being true to our word.

Action is what gives substance to our intentions. No meaningful difference exists between someone who makes time every day to ponder the importance of having integrity and someone who never gives it a moment's thought, if neither individual actually lives with integrity. The good news is that the opportunity to make choices in line with your values is ever present. Your ability to make a value-driven choice today has absolutely nothing to do with whether it's the thousandth time you've made that choice or the first.

Darrah's friend Laura told her of a revelation she had around the issue of honesty and living the commitment of honesty. Laura stated, "I always thought that because I was basically a good person, definitely not a bad person, I could do certain things without their meaning much about me. For example, I was dating two guys at once, and because I never explicitly said I was being monogamous, I told myself I wasn't being dishonest. But was I being honest within each relationship? What were my actions saying? Anyway, I realized my actions didn't sit well with *me*, because they indicated that I was invested in a relationship with each man, regardless of what I was or wasn't saying. After that, I had the realization that one isn't either an honest or a dishonest person, but rather one either is or isn't *living* honestly." Laura then made a choice about living her intention and let each man know she was dating the other. This action was consistent with her chosen intention to live honestly.

You can choose your intentions, too. The key is to follow these chosen intentions with action. Alfred Adler, the famous psychologist, once said, "Trust only movement. Life happens at the level of events not of words."

PRACTICE COMMITTED ACTION

Take pen and paper, and jot down two or three of the things that matter most to you in your relationship. Then imagine that an alien from outer space has come to visit, and your task is to describe these important things, but you can only do it by describing actions. That is, the alien doesn't understand concepts (for example, the concept of values), only actions. Write down two or three actions that help the alien understand each of the things that matter most to you in your relationship. When you've listed these, commit to doing one action a day for the next week. In fact, why not do one a day for the rest of your life?

32

COURAGEOUS LOVING

Courage is being scared to death, but saddling up anyway.
—JOHN WAYNE

Because courage is considered an asset, it has become associated with strength. Likewise, because emotions such as fear, anxiety, and feeling vulnerable are often considered signs of weakness, we equate courage with the absence of those feelings. We think that having courage means we aren't afraid. In truth, courage is all about fear and anxiety; it's about taking action despite our feelings of fear. The Latin root for the word "courage" is *cor*, which means "heart." So we're speaking of courage as the ability to take actions from the heart, even though fear may be present.

When does courage show up in relationships? From the very beginning; from the moment you risk being vulnerable, at least enough to indicate interest. From the moment you choose to reveal yourself without knowing how you'll be received, even if it's degree by tiny degree, or dare to commit to a future together without knowing what that future entails. Unless you have access to some kind of guaranteed process we don't know about, relationships always involve a leap of faith. That leap is all about courage.

At times, the mettle of your relationship will be tested. Hardship, tragedy, loss, and betrayal can cause a relationship to fall apart—or not. Although you have little or no control over such life events, what happens next is influenced hugely by the choices you make. Doggedly making one choice after another based upon your values—in other words, consistently taking committed action— will guide you steadily and surely through even the most troubled of times. And this takes heart.

We know a couple, Dan and Sheree, who experienced every parent's nightmare: the death of a child. Their four-year-old daughter, Anna, ran out in the street in front of their home and was struck and killed by a car. Along with the overwhelming devastation of this loss, each parent struggled with excruciating thoughts and feelings of guilt and blame. Dan felt responsible, because he'd been out front watering the lawn and "should" have been watching Anna more closely. He felt he should have been able to prevent this from happening. At the same time, he had secret feelings of blame toward Sheree for not doing a better job of teaching Anna how to cross the street. He also resented that she had been in the house talking on the phone instead of watching Anna. Even though he judged himself severely for having these thoughts, telling himself he was being irrational and unfair to Sheree, he had them anyway.

Sheree had the converse set of feelings. She blamed herself for not stopping Anna from running into the street, for not teaching her to be careful, for feeling happy as she chatted on the phone, and so on. She blamed Dan for not watching Anna more carefully, and herself for having terrible thoughts about Dan when he was so devastated by what happened. And even though both knew Anna had darted in front of the car, they blamed the driver who struck and killed her. So, on top of their heartbreaking loss, Dan and Sheree struggled with all sorts of unwanted thoughts and feelings, adding struggle to the struggle.

As they mourned their loss, Dan and Sheree made some choices toward courageous loving. Dan took the risk to tell his wife how he really felt, and Sheree had the courage to really listen, although much of it was hard to hear. Despite feeling overcome with sorrow, each determined to continue being loving toward the other, to see the other's pain with empathy. They ignored their listlessness and entered therapy to work though their loss, because despite it all, they valued the life they had built together and wanted to make their marriage work. Although both wanted to put their hands over their ears and shut their eyes to the world, they began to do life-affirming things: a dinner out with friends, a drive to the beach.

Neither Dan nor Sheree felt much enthusiasm for a future without their daughter, but they were willing to take small steps forward anyway. Perhaps the greatest act of courage was their decision a couple of years later to conceive another child. They understood the risk they would be taking in daring to love someone so much once again. In short, they chose to live with courage, rather than turn their backs on life in bitterness and sorrow.

PRACTICE COURAGE

Alice Mackenzie Swaim writes, "Courage is not the towering oak that sees storms come and go. It is the fragile blossom that opens in the snow." Where and when do you open, even though it feels really hard to do so? Would you be willing to challenge yourself a little in the service of courage? Find a place where you feel fear in your relationship. Ask yourself, "What does my heart really want here?" See if you could take an action, even a small one, that's about living courageously, about following your heart in your relationship. If it's consistent with what you value, take that action.

33

TRUSTING AND BEING TRUSTWORTHY

You can't shake hands with a clenched fist.—INDIRA GANDHI

What a challenge relationships can be. Even though it's incredibly empowering to recognize that we all have the ability to create the sort of relationship we want, the flip side of this freedom is that *we* (not our partner) are on the hook for how our lives are lived. As one of our friends put it, "I hate how ultimately everything is up to me." This sort of thought often comes up when someone shakes our trust, when something really wrong has occurred. Yet, what to do next is still up to us. Of course, we can remain focused on our feelings of being wronged, hurt, or righteously indignant. But that doesn't sound much like vital living, does it?

You can play two parts with respect to how trust works in your relationship. One is the degree to which you trust your partner; the other is the degree to which you are trustworthy. Notice that we're treating trust here as a way of being rather than as a quality or object that either is or isn't present. Did you wake up one morning and find something called "trust" suddenly inside you? Did your partner hand trust over to you at some point?

We speak of having our trust broken by someone. How does that work? Our trust is now damaged, so if we were to open up and look inside, we would see little broken bits of trust? No, trust is an action; it's a dynamic between you and your partner that's represented by deeds, by trusting and trustworthy actions.

To be trustworthy means to stand firm, like a tree. Trust, dependability, and reliability are all interrelated and point to staying the course in some way. When you are trustworthy, you remain firm in your commitments, firm in backing up your words. You hold steady despite hardship and fear.

What do you find trustworthy about your partner? In what ways are you trustworthy? Can your partner depend on you at all times or only at certain times? Are you reliable? When you say you're going to do something, do you do it? When you speak, do you mean it? Being trustworthy is not a destination you reach or something you acquire. Rather, it's on ongoing process made up of actions that either are or aren't trustworthy. In a sense, this is good news, because you can't blow your opportunity to be trustworthy, no matter how badly you have let your partner down. The bad news is that there's no such thing as an inconsequential transgression. When you choose to forget a promise you've made, you're intentionally choosing to lay aside being trustworthy. In that moment, you cannot be trusted, regardless of who you have been in the past or who you might be tomorrow. You have stepped off your valued path. What do you do when you have stepped off the path? Why, you step right back on!

And trusting your partner is your choice, as well. Your partner will act in all sorts of ways that seem trustworthy, and some that won't. Your work on trusting your partner involves openness and a willingness to have faith in your partner. In short, although it might seem easier to leave trustworthiness completely up to your partner, the fact is that you have a great deal of power when it comes to the trust in your relationship. If you value trust, we encourage you to begin building it, brick by mighty brick.

PRACTICE TRUST

In what ways do you demonstrate being trustworthy in your relationship? In what ways do you demonstrate being trusting? In what ways do your actions fall more into the "not trustworthy" category? If you value being trustworthy in your relationship, how might you alter your actions to be more in line with this value?

34

THE POWER OF FORGIVENESS

Anger makes you smaller, while forgiveness forces you to grow beyond what you were. —CHERIE CARTER-SCOTT

What happens when trust is betrayed? How do we forgive? *Should* we forgive? Before tackling the topics of transgression and forgiveness, it's important to move out of any debate about right and wrong. The opportunity to take committed action supersedes past rights and wrongs; it rises above and remains untouched by what has gone before. Our values point the way, and committed action takes us there. So, let's look at how this works in a situation in which forgiveness is on the line. Suppose you're in a committed, monogamous marriage and your spouse has an affair. Along with all your thoughts and feelings, you have many choices: Do you leave the relationship? If so, when? Do you stay? If so, how? Do you forgive? What if you don't feel forgiving but want to keep the relationship—what do you do with those feelings of distrust?

Much as you might wish for a stone tablet to fall out of the sky and tell you what to do in this situation, the choice is yours. What won't work, however, is to wait until your feelings go away before choosing. The feelings will come and go. Let's say you choose to stay and rebuild the relationship, and many years go by. Even if those years turn out to be mostly good and loving, when you think back on the time of betrayal, painful feelings are likely to show up. They belong to the experience. Although you may think it is your partner's job to fix your feelings of hurt and distrust, that's not true. "But," you protest, "it's her fault I feel this way!" Or you argue, "I don't trust him anymore. He needs to prove to me he's trustworthy, then *maybe* I'll trust him again."

Let's look more closely at what it takes to fix this situation. Suppose your partner is full of remorse and begs for forgiveness. That may mollify you, but it won't erase the hurt. You may feel comforted in the moment, but if you revisit the betrayal in your mind, up come the feelings of hurt. Most likely, what you really want is a guarantee that you won't be hurt again. But even if your partner promises up and down that there will be no future transgression, how will you know for sure? Besides, your partner could devote himself or herself to never hurting you like that again, and then get run over by a bus. Wham! There's hurt once again. So, all this is to make the point that what's needed here doesn't rest with having your partner pass some sort of test. If your value is to remain in a relationship despite a breach of trust, it's up to you whether to risk forgiving, given that the future is unknown and life's pains can't be prevented with promises or guarantees.

This is where forgiveness is needed. "Forgiveness" literally means to "give what went before." Notice that it's a giving, not a feeling. You may feel a sense of lightness or relief along with forgiveness. As with all other emotions, this sense of lightness will come and go. The action is in the giving—giving back to your partner what was there before the hurt, treating your partner *as if* the transgression didn't happen. It's important to keep in mind that this is a process, not an outcome. It doesn't mean that you suddenly go back to treating your partner as you did prior to the affair but, rather, that you commit to work on it. You can take daily actions that look like the actions you took before the affair. In fact, you can even improve on these actions.

Here's an example. Zoe and Aaron had been married for ten years when he had an affair. Although Zoe was very bitter about it, she made the decision to stay in the relationship. However, she decided not to forgive. She felt exceedingly wronged and made sure her husband remembered this. She continued to punish him and give him the very cold shoulder for two years. This took a lot of effort on her part and turned out to be not much fun. At last, she began to realize how unhappy this was making her and how intolerable the relationship had become. She realized she was punishing herself; she was taking the poison and waiting for the other guy to die.

Forgiveness truly was the place Zoe needed to go. She needed to pursue it as an action rather than waiting for it to develop as a feeling. She chose to start by making one little act of forgiveness. She gave her husband back his kiss good night. Later, she added a friendly smile and hug in the morning. Then she was willing to sit next to him on the couch, and so on. She didn't always feel great about these actions, but she used them as medicine to repair the relationship. Eventually these small acts of forgiveness added up, and she once again felt *in* her marriage.

We have focused on the big stuff, such as betrayal and infidelity; however, forgiveness applies to the little stuff, as well. Whether it is a hurtful comment, a forgotten task or anniversary, or embarrassing public behavior, it's possible to give back what was there before the harm. The question is, will you choose it? And then, will you do it? Such giving can create something very powerful in your relationship. It can give you renewed intimacy. You create not only an opening for you and your partner to move out of being stuck but also a way to grow and to move into new possibilities in your relationship. Forgiveness is a perfect gift for the partner with whom you plan to spend your life.

PRACTICE FORGIVENESS

Have you ever forgiven someone and experienced a feeling of relief, only to discover, when you thought about it later that, that you felt mad again? Yeah, that's happened to us, too. This is why the action of forgiveness is so powerful—it doesn't depend on the emotional roller-coaster settling down in order for it to work. Stop and consider whether you're still keeping your partner on the hook about something that happened in the past, something that you haven't let go of, but could let go of now. Ask yourself what would happen if you let your partner off the hook. What might be different for you and for your partner? Take one small action today to create that opening.

35

COMMITTED FRIENDS

A friend is one who knows us, but loves us anyway.
—FR. JEROME CUMMINGS

Noted couples researcher John Gottman reports that after many years of studying marriages, he can tell within five minutes of observing a couple while they argue whether the relationship will end in divorce (Gottman and Silver 1999). A key predictor, he says, is the presence of contempt. Perhaps this is because when contempt enters, the ability to recognize the basic value of our partner is compromised.

Friendship is the opposite of contempt. Whereas contempt is about scorn, friendship is about recognizing another's inherent, fundamental value. It's about liking our partner, in spite of his or her quirks. The bond of friendship is not only essential to a loving and vital relationship but also its greatest reward.

Think about your best friend, aside from your partner. What feels particularly good about that relationship? Probably it's the comforting sense of being liked, of being valued simply for who you are, or perhaps despite all that you are. Good friendships give us a sense of ease, a sense that we are okay, even with all our warts and foibles. A friendship is therefore defined by how each person regards the other, which is demonstrated by how they treat one another. True friendship involves an agreement to treat one another with the respect and courtesy due someone of value.

Ask yourself whether you treat your partner as you would a friend. For instance, if a friend were in the habit of forgetting to go to the dry cleaners, would you be compelled to point this out? You might notice it or have thoughts and judgments about it, but you'd probably choose not to say anything out of respect for the relationship, or because you didn't to want make your friend unnecessarily unhappy. Being friends doesn't grant us an open invitation to offer our thoughts and opinions about each other's behavior. Why would this be different in an intimate relationship? It's interesting how easily we lose sight of the possibility for genuine friendship with our partner. Sadly, we lose sight of how to *be* a friend in what's actually our most important and intimate relationship.

This issue of judgment is worth exploring more fully. Let's say, for example, that your friend Jill can be a little testy when stressed. Do you notice a bit more willingness to say to yourself, "Well, that's just the way Jill is" and to move on, rather than fixating on how Jill needs to change, as you might with your spouse? Many people find that they have less judgment in their relationships with friends than they do with a partner. Although it may be difficult to get away from expectations and judgments with a partner, the result is a lesser degree of friendship in that relationship.

Think about the elements of friendship that are most important to you. Perhaps one element is a sense of being understood. How do you demonstrate being understanding of your partner? Perhaps it's being supportive. In what ways do you actively support your partner? Our friend Beth told us that what she loved most about her close friends was their ability to celebrate her successes with her. She said, "When they're almost happier than I am that something is going well for me, I know that that's true friendship." She also said, "A true friend, however, also joins me when things aren't going well." Do you actively share in your partner's joys as well as his or her sorrows?

So, think about the ways in which your actions are or are not in the service of friendship. We have so many golden opportunities to respond with a gentle laugh of understanding instead of censure. We have the chance to say, "I understand," rather than to correct. We have the opportunity to support and encourage. If you consider your relationship with your partner a valuable friendship, consider how you can nurture it and make it stronger. Look for an opportunity today. Take it and see what happens next!

PRACTICE FRIENDSHIP

As you engage with your partner, try to catch yourself in a given moment and ask if you'd be doing something differently if this were a friend instead of your partner. Would you have said what you just said in a different way? Would you have made the request you just made? Would you have responded differently to something your partner said or did? Now see if you can stop yourself in the moment *before* you act, and adjust your behavior to fit how you would be with a friend. Try to do this at least once per day for the next week.

36

ROMANTICALLY COMMITTED

*Love is like a violin; the music may stop now and then, but the
strings remain forever.*—JUNE MASTERS BACHER

Where has the romance gone? Interesting question! We look
at romance as a *thing* that can be misplaced, like a set of
keys. We treat it like something tangible that dwindled away, like
last year's box of Valentine's Day chocolates. But how does that
work? When you remember the romance you "used to have" in your
relationship, where was it? Perhaps you think of it as a small heart-
shaped mass that resided somewhere inside you both. Or perhaps
it was a blushing aura around your heads or something nestled
mischievously under your pillows. Of course not, you say. But then,

what *do* you mean when you say, "We just don't have the romance anymore"? What has actually been lost?

Romance, as a feeling, is a wonderful, tingle-to-your-toes experience that comes and goes like any other feeling. It also can refer to an action, such as when you're doing something romantic. Ah, that's interesting. When you were acting, or *being*, romantic in the past, what were you doing? If you're *feeling* romantic right now, what are you doing? Maybe it never occurred to you that it's possible to *feel* romantic but not *be* romantic. Is romance a feeling or an action?

Fortunately, we have the ability to be romantic regardless of how we feel in the moment. As June Masters Bacher said, even if we don't hear its music all the time, we still have the instrument of love. We can pick it up and play it whenever we choose. Once romantic actions are back in a relationship, romance can happen.

Think back to something you experienced in your life that you found romantic. What would you say was the most romantic experience you've ever had? See if you can pick out the specific actions that created that experience. Notice that this can include both grand and simple gestures. For example, one that comes to Darrah's mind is the time her college boyfriend gave her candy to support her during finals week. Knowing that she loved Starburst candy (except the lime-green ones), he gave her a huge jar of them, with all the green ones taken out. In another instance, she received a mysterious call to "meet me in the rose garden at midnight." When she got there, she found a midnight picnic, complete with champagne. In each of these instances, her boyfriend's actions created an experience to remember. You can do the same with your partner, and you can do it today!

PRACTICE ROMANCE

Be the ultimate romantic. Imagine for a moment that you're one of the most romantic persons on the planet, and you are in your relationship of choice. What choices would you make, and how would you *be* in that relationship? How might you bring this into your current relationship?

Take romantic action. Think back to a time when your relationship seemed romantic. List three things you did relationshipwise during that time, actions that represent romance to you. Now pick one and commit to doing that action before the end of the day. Note that your ability to do this doesn't rest on how you are feeling. If, in fact, you value romance, being romantic is well within your power.

Conclusion

You picked up this book for a reason. Perhaps something about the title or jacket caught your eye; perhaps you'd heard of acceptance and commitment therapy and wondered how it might help your relationship. You might be happy in your relationship and looking for a way to enhance it, or unhappy in your relationship and looking for answers. Either way, we suspect something more fundamental is at work here. That is to say, as a human being, in your heart of hearts, you long for connection in the most intimate way—a way that says, "Yes, you're okay; you have value exactly as you are." At their best, intimate relationships offer each of us basic validation for who we are and how we want to be in the world. To serve as a partner and witness another's life enhances our life experience. Herein lies a wellspring of riches: companionship, friendship, passion, support, and devotion, to name a few.

The mistake so many of us make is to go in search of a golden egg, acutely aware of what we are missing as we pick our way through one relationship after another. In fact, what we're missing is our ability to create a relationship that's about vital loving, passion, support, devotion, and so on. Is that too much work? Not if you remember that vitality comes from loving, not just from being loved. Unfortunately, many go their entire lives without experiencing what is truly possible when it comes to love. Why don't you find out differently? Start from a place of deep acceptance of yourself and your partner as 100 percent whole just as you are. Next, determine what you value most about your relationship, and let it be that. There's no need for your partner to do x, y, or z—you be the one. Go love your partner, and do it today!

REFERENCES

Achebe, Chinua. 1967. *Arrow of God*. New York: John Day.

Buss, David M. 2003. *The Evolution of Desire: Strategies of Human Mating*. New York: Basic Books.

Gottman, John M., Julie S. Gottman, and Joan DeClaire. 2006. *Ten Lessons to Transform Your Marriage*. New York: Three Rivers Press.

Gottman, John. M., and Nan Silver. 1999. *The Seven Principles for Making Marriage Work*. New York: Three Rivers Press.

Hayes, Steven. C., Kirk D. Strosahl, and Kelly G. Wilson. 1999. *Acceptance and Commitment Therapy: An Experiential Approach to Behavior Change*. New York: The Guilford Press.

Kohut, Heinz. 1984. *How Does Analysis Cure?* Chicago: University of Chicago Press.

Laumann, Edward O., John H. Gagnon, Robert T. Michael, and Stuart Michaels. 1994. *The Social Organization of Sexuality: Sexual Practices in the United States.* Chicago: University of Chicago Press.

Luoma, Jason B., Steven C. Hayes, and Robyn D. Walser. 2007. *Learning Acceptance and Commitment Therapy: A Skills Training Workbook For Therapists.* Oakland, CA: New Harbinger Publications.

Peck, M. Scott 1978. *The Road Less Traveled.* New York: Simon & Schuster.

Wolfers, Justin. 2008. Misreporting on divorce. *New York Times*, March 21, Opinion section. http://freakonomics.blogs.nytimes .com/2008/03/21/misreporting-on-divorce/ (accessed July 5, 2008).

Robyn D. Walser, Ph.D., is a psychologist who works as a consultant, workshop presenter, and therapist in her private business, TL Consultation Services. She also works at the National Center for PTSD in the Veterans Affairs Palo Alto Health Care System in California. She received her doctorate in clinical psychology from the University of Nevada, Reno, and has clinical and research expertise in traumatic stress, substance abuse, and acceptance and commitment therapy (ACT). She is an internationally recognized trainer in ACT and has co-authored journal articles, book chapters, and two books on this intervention.

Darrah Westrup, Ph.D., is a clinical psychologist with the National Center for PTSD at the Veterans Affairs Palo Alto Health Care System in California. She serves as attending psychologist at the Women's Trauma Recovery Program, a ten-bed, sixty-day residential treatment program for women veterans with military-related PTSD. She is also program director of the Outpatient Women's Mental Health Center. Westrup received her graduate degree from West Virginia University and completed her postdoctoral fellowship in the behavioral medicine department at Stanford University. She has clinical and research expertise in the areas of PTSD, substance abuse, stalking behavior, and experiential avoidance as it relates to psychological dysfunction.

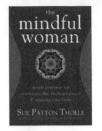